# LOOKING Beyond

*by*

Christopher J Gammon

A CIP catalogue record is available for this book from the British Library.

ISBN: 978-1-5262-0176-8

Designed by Impression Print and Design
Printed and bound in the United Kingdom by
Impression Print and Design
24 Carden Avenue
Brighton
BN1 8NA

Distributed by
Christopher J Gammon
125 Braeside Avenue
Brighton
BN1 8SQ

Tel: 01273 233277
Email: christopher125@ntlworld.com

# ABOUT THE AUTHOR

Christopher Gammon has been a Spiritualist for over forty years. He trained, alongside his wife, Linda, as a healer at The Sanctuary of Progress run by Medium Linda Codling and her husband Keith.

Christopher and Linda were founder members of The Fountain Group, (now Fountain International), where they learned to dowse for energies and ley lines. This proved to be useful in putting right the energies in homes. To date, he has presided over more than a hundred house realignments with his team.

Christopher and Linda developed their mediumship with local mediums. Unfortunately, Linda died in 2002, at the age of fifty-five. Christopher continued to develop his mediumship and has worked on spiritualist platforms as a medium and as a speaker; he is noted for his own brand of philosophy.

Christopher has been a musician since junior school and trained as a music teacher between 1975 and 1979. His hobbies are singing and rock climbing on the sandstone outcrops in North Sussex and Kent.

# ACKNOWLEDGEMENTS

My thanks are due to Jane Lang and Valerie Vivaud for reading the first and subsequent drafts of my book and for their positive comments.

Thanks also due to Dorothy Young for her help, with her husband, Alan, in getting it published.

Thanks are also due to those from whom I have learned a great deal over the years; principally, Keith and Linda Codling, who ran The Sanctuary of Progress where I trained as a healer and began my psychic development. I was also the House Realignments officer at the sanctuary.

John Carroll ran the first really serious circle in which I sat, so, thank you John for helping me on my way. Thanks are due to Betty Horne in whose circle I honed my skills in teaching philosophy and also to Lynn Probert and Eamonn Downey, whose mediumship and excellent teaching skills took me, and so many others to new heights in mediumship.

Thanks also to the presidents of Brighton churches who have allowed me to work on their platforms: Joan Bygrave, Deborah Knowles and Gordon Harley. Being a speaker on their platforms has allowed me to formulate my philosophies.

Thanks also to all of the tutors at The Arthur Findlay College in whose groups I have been to learn about trance mediumship.

# CONTENTS

# INTRODUCTION

I have spent many years in spiritualist churches listening to speakers and demonstrators, (mediums) giving messages and philosophies. The point that has struck me most over all these years is the fact that most of the speakers have had a limited vision of what life in spirit is all about and a limited knowledge of things spiritual. We are all limited by our knowledge, but the point that I am trying to make is that, in answer to any particular question, the answer, most often, is defined in only one area.

An example of this is: if a child dies and goes to the spirit realms, that child will, "grow-up in spirit". The words between the apostrophes are the actual words, which I have heard many times. It forgets the spiritualist principle that, "Life is eternal". The child might have actually had more incarnations on the Earth-plane than its parents. It might well be a very old soul who has touched the Earth in this incarnation to teach the parents a significant lesson. Perhaps, that of mourning the loss of a child, and then getting on with their lives.

I would also take to task those mediums who have given messages to the effect that one mustn't grieve too much for a passed love one because, "Your grief is holding them back". This means that, because of your distress at your loss, your loved ones hover around you to try to comfort you and, thus, you hold up their spiritual progress. Again, I feel like screaming out, "We are eternal beings, does it matter that our loved one is spending time with us? They have eternity in which to develop". (The 7th Spiritualist principle is: Eternal progress open to every human soul). The same medium will tell you that, "There is no time in Spirit". It seems to me that they don't think things through or make connections. Their thinking is compartmentalised and they often contradict themselves from one address to the next.

This book, therefore, sets out to give broader views of many aspects of spiritual philosophy.

I hasten to point out that I have, (but rarely), heard speakers who have pointed out different scenarios with reference to particular aspects.

In reading the following chapters, it is necessary to accept that we come to the Earth-plane for many reasons in order to obtain Soul growth. It is also necessary to accept that we come to the Earth-plane many times before we can learn all that we have to learn; i.e., to have a belief in reincarnation. It is not reasonable to assume that we can achieve the wealth of experience and knowledge that is available in one short lifetime.

However, our lives on Earth are not just about learning lessons, often they are about building our spiritual character, giving us inner strength and determination. It is difficult for me to accept the premise, voiced by many, that our spirit selves have all the knowledge before we descend to the material vibration. It makes no sense at all, to me, that we are made to forget this knowledge in order to learn it all again in our fleshly bodies. However, it is true to say that all knowledge is available in the Halls of Knowledge but not all knowledge is available to us in our present state of spiritual evolution.

Wherever I've been in Spiritualist gatherings, I've found people who think they have the answer to everything; gained from the philosophies handed down by guides such as Silver Birch and White Eagle. For me, these philosophies are the starting point not the end product. Every situation is different depending upon the people involved in the situation. We cannot say, "This has happened, so it is meant to be." Our correct response should be, "This has happened, where do we go from here?"

I do not expect everyone, or anyone, to agree with everything I have to say. My purpose in writing this book is to get people to think beyond what they have been given and to form their own ideas and philosophies.

The book is in three sections: Spiritual Philosophy, Spiritual knowledge and Developing mediumship.

# CHAPTER ONE

## CHILDREN PASSING INTO SPIRIT

It is appropriate to begin with the point discussed in the introduction: that of a child going into spirit.

Many years ago, I had the unpleasant experience of going to the funeral of a child. The funeral was held on what would have been her second birthday.

My wife and I were horrified at the Methodist funeral to hear the minister say that he could offer no explanation as to why such things happen. Had he been a Spiritualist minister he could have offered several explanations. Sadly, none that would have immediately consoled the grieving parents.

As I said in the introduction, one reason for her death could have been a lesson for the parents to learn: that, no matter how great the loss, "Life goes on". Happily, the parents did move on and had further children. The loss is still carried in the heart but does not stop them from living.

Compare their story to other people whom I knew who lost a child who was just seven years old.

These parents were so devastated that they did, in fact, stop their life in its tracks and the child's room was kept as a shrine for some years and both parents stopped work and spent their time sitting around the house caught up in their grief; this went on for several years. Happily, they did eventually go forward on their pathways.

Another possible reason for such a short life could be that the previous incarnation of the child had been cut short by the taking of its own life. I say, possible, because this is one theory but I have heard many mediums bring a spirit forward who says that they, now, regret taking their own lives but they are fine and happy now. In this case, the spirit could be persuaded by its guides that it was necessary to come back to the Earth plane to fulfil its allotted time-span and, maybe, to undergo the suffering which caused it to hasten its journey into Spirit.

Sometimes, parents are inspired by their experience, to get involved with, or set-up, associations dealing with the same problems that they underwent, in order to help other families to cope with similar situations.

Of course, it is not only family and friends who are involved. There are experiences for doctors, nurses and all sorts of support groups who can, by virtue of the work they do, experience love and compassion as well as seeing the suffering, which sick children undergo. They can also experience the bravery and composure shown by these children in their adversity.

The spirit of the child might have elected to go through the experience for its own spiritual development. Not just to undergo the physical and emotional trauma of the experience but also to experience the love, care and compassion that parents, family members, friends and their carers can direct towards it.

Such experiences, we are told, are supposed to make us stronger. As someone who has lost a very loved wife, I immediately took-up life again. This is not to say that I didn't have times on my own where I sobbed out my grief, but I knew that despite her physical absence, we would never be parted spiritually.

This leads me on to the question that I have heard posed by people who have had more than one partner and might well be the only survivor of several marriages: "Which of my husbands, or wives, will I be with when I return to Spirit?"

Although the nearest planes to the Earth plane are very similar and people can live lives very much as they did on Earth, there are important differences. For example, when we go to Spirit, we can be conscious of a much wider grouping of relationships. We have to remember that most of us have had previous lives and have had previous partners in those life times. So it is not just a question of "Which partner of this life time will I be with" but, really a question of "With whom am I most compatible"?

On leaving the Earth-plane, we are free to choose with whom we will be. It's a question of "Birds of a feather."


## RELATIONSHIPS IN SPIRIT

Many people worry about whether or not they will be with their earthly partner when they go into Spirit. If you haven't been compatible with your partner, you will not be with them in the Spirit World. You will be with those only of a similar vibration to yourself.

On entering the spirit realms, we will naturally be met by those who loved us most in the incarnation we have just left. Our husbands, wives, partners, fathers, mothers and other friends and family. However, we will also be met by our eternal spiritual partner who we will recognise instantly. That does depend, of course, on whether they are in the Spirit world and not on the Earth-plane. When we have settled in more and we begin to access the memories of past lives, loved-ones from those past lives will join us.

In my present lifetime, I have been conscious of the fact that few people marry their spiritual 'other half'. Many are here to experience the opposite of an ideal relationship, with all the hardships and emotional problems, which this can cause. It all comes down to the basic reason that we come to the Earth-plane: to undergo experiences, which will help us to evolve spiritually and enhance our spiritual vibration.

My wife and I were very close and were told by our friend and medium, Linda Codling, that we were twin souls. We were so close in everything that we did and thought that we thought of ourselves as "One spirit in two bodies". Many mediums have described us as "Two peas in a pod".

It came as a huge surprise to me, therefore, that when I met someone a few years after my wife's death and began a relationship with her, I felt a closeness of vibration that I couldn't explain. This was a question for my guides to answer.

I was told that, although Linda and I were twin souls, we were part of a much larger group whose vibrations were very close. Linda and I are a perfect match but there are other souls with whom I am very closely aligned vibrationally. Although I had heard about group souls coalescing in ever larger groups, this twin soul grouping was something I hadn't considered very closely. How many other souls there are with whom I have such a close vibration, I really cannot say.

My wife, Linda, used to say that sometime in the future, we would merge our souls into one. I said earlier that we belong to a group of souls. As we progress spiritually and our vibrations match more and more closely, I believe that we do merge with others to become more complete.

I would like to give an analogy here: imagine that the whole of Creation is a giant jigsaw puzzle where all the parts of the puzzle have to fit exactly with those around it. Now zoom in to a scene upon the Earth plane; all the parts fit together in groups: trees, grass, birds, a stream, the Sky etc. The pieces of each object are intrinsically, a part of that object. The parts of the tree fit together, the parts of the sky fit together etc. All the pieces within the tree are in close relationship and, owing to the way in which the pieces are cut, certain pieces will only fit with certain other pieces. Thus, harmony is created by fitting the exactly right pieces together.

# CHAPTER TWO

## SPIRIT REALMS

The number of spirit realms is infinite. There are definitely more than the "Seven" realms beloved by so many. I was taught that there are thirteen realms close to the Earth-plane and beyond these, another thirteen, and beyond these and so on.

The realms closest to us in vibration are very much like our own world excepting that whatever exists there is created by thought. (This is true of our own realm in as much as everything that is made is preceded by thought). For example, if you want a cottage in the country with roses round the door, you just think it into existence. However, for those who are the least spiritually developed, their world is created for them and they live lives much as they did on the Earth-plane. One can eat, drink, make love and do all the things that are possible on the material plane.

It is important to remember that within any particular realm, everything is 'solid' to everything else, just as it is on this plane. This is because everything and everyone is vibrating within a limited range of vibration. Some people recently have been saying that Spirit do not have bodies; that they are just energy or light. This is total nonsense; some mediums are known to be able to see Spirit objectively; i.e. with their eyes. I myself have been privileged to see a spirit objectively on one occasion. Arthur Findlay, one of Spiritualism's great figures says, in one of his books, that Spirit have bodies which are identical to their physical counterpart. We all know that when we die, our spirit leaves the body in its etheric body. We think that our earth is the most dense realm but this is not necessarily true. Remembering that which has been said previously, that everything in a particular realm is solid to all that is in that realm, it is possible that there are denser worlds than ours; particularly when you know that there are realms which we would call dark, (darker than ours), and are inhabited by those which we would call sub-human or base.

The Christian church talks of Heaven as being above us. So many people, whom I have met, think that it is up in the Sky somewhere.

The Spirit world is all around us. It interpenetrates our material world. It is at a much higher vibration than the material plane, which is why it cannot, usually, be seen.

# ARRIVAL IN SPIRIT

I must say, before talking about this that when someone that you love is very ill and certain to die, you should let them go. Many people, selfishly, cling on to their loved one, because they either don't want to lose them or are afraid of what might be going to happen to them when they get to the spirit realms.

Thus, sometimes the terminally ill person hangs about the earth plane in great pain and discomfort for the benefit of those left behind. When my wife knew that her passing was inevitable, she told all of the doctors, nurses and hospice staff the she was going to die, and to get it over with as soon as possible. I was asked by one of the staff at the hospice, what I thought and, although I didn't want to lose her, I knew that I would like her pain and discomfort to end as soon as possible. "I agree with her" was my reply.

"So many people cling to their loved ones", she told me, despite the pain which they are suffering. If someone is terminal, I like to think that they would pass to the spirit world sooner rather than later.

Before one arrives in Spirit, one has to die, or, rather, the body has to die in order for the spirit to be released (Some people think of this as the spirit shedding the body). This can be a sudden, dramatic event or a gradual, almost evolutionary process.

In the case of a person who has a long term illness resulting in death or just dies from old age, the spirit is prepared over a period of months, or longer, to adjust to the change of home. People often drift in and out of the body at this time; sometimes meeting loved ones on the other side.

This is why they begin to talk about relatives or friends already gone to Spirit. During this period of adjustment, the aura is given, (by Spirit), healing layers, in which the soul can bask and so help the passing. When the spirit is resting in one of these layers, it is possible for the person to receive the words that loved-ones on the Earth plane are saying and to feel the love-vibration given-off as they sit with them holding hands etc.

In the above case, the spirit does not need the adjustment of a spirit catapulted into Spirit by an accident or has had traumatic experiences prior to entry. The slowly adjusted spirit can settle into Spirit very quickly and knows immediately where they are. They are met by their loved-ones as they leave the body and can feel straight away the joy that is abundant in the spirit realms.

In other cases, adjustment is often longer and, in some cases, Earth-bound spirits can be roaming the material plains for a very long time. Such was the case of my mother-in-law. My wife and I were members of a group of leyline energy workers called "The Fountain Group" (More later). One of the members of this group was Betty Shine, a well-known medium and author of spiritual books. During a group meeting, one day, Betty took me aside and told me that my wife, Linda, was being influenced by an Earth-bound spirit who didn't accept the sort of teaching that we were getting through the Fountain Group, or the philosophy taught at Spiritualist churches. She didn't tell me who it was but I found out for myself.

One evening, having just got into bed, I was aware that the spirit of Linda's mother, Muriel, was present. I immediately asked for my guides to come in and to escort her into Spirit, where she belonged. I was aware of her distress as they took her away.

When Linda came in to go to bed, I told her what had happened and told her what Betty had told me. This event was confirmed by a medium a few months later and I did receive a message of thanks from Muriel at a later date. From this time on, Linda began to embrace the teachings of Spiritualism.

Many years later, when I was doing house energy realignments and removing Earth-bound spirits to spirit realms, a number of people asked me not to remove their "ghost" because they liked having them there.

I told them, of course, that when people die, it is right and proper for them to go to spirit and that it is their natural home. They can live a sort of nightmarish existence on the material plane and are distressed. It is selfish to want to have the kudos of having your own pet ghost.

Usually, the reason for a spirit being Earth-bound is through some trauma or other or because they feel unable to leave behind someone whom they love. This was so in Muriel's case. She had died of cancer in a London hospital and Linda was unable to visit her before she died. Linda was very young when we married and Muriel, like any mother, was very concerned about looking after her daughter. Unfortunately, this resulted in her being stranded on the Earth-plane for thirteen years.

Newly arrived spirits who have had long illnesses often awake to find themselves in a hospital, where they are cared for by trained staff, until such time as they can be told that they are on the "other side". They are gradually introduced to the idea that they are in Spirit and are then allowed to have visits from their "already departed" loved ones.

Spirit hospitals are places where new entrants to the spirit world can receive care. They would have experienced physical suffering on the Earth-plane or would have died in an accident and, perhaps, not be aware of where they were. As they recover and become aware of their status, their loved ones in Spirit would begin to visit them.

As has been said before, there are different circumstances leading to the passing over into the spirit world.

Most of the mediums, if not all, have stated that children grow-up in Spirit. Often, they have presented the spirit of a child as of the age that it would have been had the child still been on the Earth-plane. For example, if a child was, say, six years old when they passed, and their passing was twelve years ago, they are presented as being of the age of eighteen. This is, of course, nonsense. The same medium will say, "There's no Time in Spirit." The Spirit is eternal and there is no time in Spirit, as we know it on the Earth-plane. Therefore, Spirit is ageless. Children, newly arriving in Spirit might take longer to adjust, than adults, however, which is why there are nurseries for them in Spirit.

We do know that some spirits present themselves as children. The world famous, Leslie Flint, had a spirit child who used to be part of his physical circle. He used to escort other spirits into the circle to speak with recipients and keep the sitters entertained with his wit. It is difficult for me to believe that "Tommy" was a young child because of the way in which he organised things. Tommy also presented himself as a cockney, which is what he chose to do. Usually, advanced spirits have had incarnations in many different nationalities and regions. And, some say, that our guides appear to us in the guise of their last earthly incarnation.

Stewart Alexander, well- known physical medium, tells of the time that someone in the circle asked a spirit, who always appeared as a young, black child if she were really a child, because, when she answered questions, she seemed to be much older. At the request of members of the circle, "Topsy" revealed herself in all her glory, (naked) to be a white, adult woman.

In the case of a child entering Spirit, it would depend on the spiritual development of the child's spirit as to whether it "grew-up" in Spirit or whether it was an advanced spirit who would go straight to the level from whence it came.

A child not so developed would, probably, after a stay in a spirit hospital, join a school grouping appropriate to its earth age on death. The child would then grow-up as it would on the Earth-plane. At some time, however, it has to be informed of its spirit state because another Earth incarnation might be appropriate.

This can vary from a few earth years to perhaps hundreds of years. It has been known for children from far back in time to visit development circles. A development circle is a group where people develop their mediumship under the watchful eye of a trained medium.

By and large, the majority of people passing over have no trouble and are met immediately by the loved ones. They usually then have a big party to celebrate the "birth into Spirit" of the newly arrived soul. Often, loved ones who proceeded them into Spirit have organised their "dream home" or whatever and they will spend time adjusting to their new state before going to examine the akashic record of the life they have just lived on the material plane.

They are joined in this by their guides; those more highly evolved spirits who were responsible for their spiritual journey. They will be able to see a "film" of their Earth-life and assess the results. There is no blame and there are no penalties. Before coming to the Earth-plane, they will have been assigned guides to help them and to advise them as to which parents to choose and which friends to make. This is important for the experiences, which they will have, and for the opportunities, which may arise for them to progress.

It is not a terrible thing if they haven't achieved their goals. There is always another opportunity to return to the material life and have another go. There was a student at the Sanctuary of Progress, (Where my wife and I were trained), who started-out very promisingly. After two years of being a model student, she decided that she could take things easy and not put herself out as much as she had previously. It was fortunate that another opportunity arose and she left before she could be "terminated". She went from place to place after this looking for a niche but never really found one. She moved away and we didn't hear news of her again.

I relate this story to show how it is possible for a spirit to fall short of their expected goals. It is, of course, possible that she did return to her pathway in later years. If not, then, on her return to Spirit, she would be shown how and where she went wrong and would be given the opportunity to have another go.

I would like to say, here, that it is also possible to exceed the goals which were set for your earthly journey, just as it is possible for people to surpass that which they thought was beyond them. Since I turned seventy years old, I have done more difficult climbing routes than I had done previously. This is because I started climbing with a new group of climbers who made me push my limits.

## WHAT CAN WE DO IN THE SPIRIT REALMS?

Basically, we can do anything that takes our fancy: painting, learn to play an instrument, learn to become a healer. All is possible in the Spirit World. I fully intend to improve my piano playing when I get to the other side and I also intend to go rock climbing, which has been one of my favourite pursuits during this lifetime.

Many people will prepare for a future incarnation on Earth; whether it is something like mediumship and healing or learning an art purely for self-pleasure. Of course, others will receive pleasure from those pursuits as well as the person who is the artist.

Others may well decide to become doctors, nurses, carers, actors singers etc. etc. All will go to the Halls of Learning where eager tutors and innumerable tomes await them.

As well as learning, one can indulge in pleasure pursuits. You can plan and build your own house and garden, visit friends in their homes; wander around lakes, parks and gardens. In fact, there is nothing that you cannot do on the earth plane, but every experience is different to that which one gets on the material plane.

Many people will ask, "How can this be, we have no bodies in the Spirit World".

My understanding is that we do have bodies; in the lower planes, they are very much like our earthly bodies. On Earth, some call these the Astral body or the Etheric Double. If Spirit did not have bodies, then materialisations in physical circles couldn't take place. This is where the medium produces ectoplasm in to which the spirit steps so that they can be seen and touched should the spirit control allow. In transfiguration, the spirit can place its face in the ectoplasm and be instantly recognised as the person known on Earth.

There are some mediums who actually see Spirit objectively; that is, not as an image in the mind but just as they can see people in the flesh. I have experienced this on just one occasion. It was totally unexpected and I wasn't looking for it. I was walking down a long corridor in a friend's house and happened to glance into a room. The spirit of a man was standing in the room and he looked as surprised as I was. I perceived him for several seconds and then he disappeared.

There was a time when I, and others were of the opinion that Spirit had no gender. I think, now, that this is not true. Indeed, I have been at a trance demonstration at the Arthur Findlay College, when a spirit has come through to say, "I am definitely male".

When I saw a spirit objectively, it was a man, dressed in a man's clothing. This being so, it is conceivable that, on the lower planes at least, children are born. I had been told at the Sanctuary of progress that new spirits are being created all the time. This could answer the questions about gender on the Earth plane; why some people born into a body of a particular gender feel, quite definitely, that they are the other gender; female spirit born into a male body and vice versa.

# CHAPTER THREE

## WHY ARE WE BORN INTO THE MATERIAL WORLD?

Many people who have come to me for healing have energy problems resulting from the over zealous care of others. They seem to spend their time worrying about their family or friends with the result that they neglect themselves. I always tell them, "The most important person in your life is you". Perhaps one of their tasks on the Earth plane is to care for others, but not to the exclusion of their own needs. One friend whom I told this, said. "I've never considered myself before".

We come to this plane for our own spiritual growth and, in the above case; such people are hindering the spiritual growth of their loved ones by taking away their responsibility for their own lives.

Before a spirit sets off to be born on the material plane, they will meet with their, soon to be, guides and helpers to discuss the aims and objectives of their new life. They might, of course, be setting-out just to experience the many delights possible through having a material body: Eating, drinking, making love, partaking in various sports activities etc. Sometimes, a spirit, having had a particularly arduous Earth incarnation, will be given an easy life where others will claim that they seem to be charmed; where everything goes right for them and nothing seems to go wrong. Spirits who have not previously incarnated upon Earth are usually given this sort of life. It's a sort of "Loss leader".

As well as discussing with your guides and advisors, you will meet some of the people with whom you will be associated in the next incarnation. Of course, it is likely that you will meet with your parents and their contemporaries before they make their journey to the Earth-plane along with, perhaps, other members of the family, but the spirit awaiting incarnation will have their own contemporaries to consider; brothers, sisters, friends, enemies workmates etc. Some of these will still be in spirit and they will be at the meeting with your guides and advisors. Not all of these spirits will be on your vibration but all will agree to help each other to learn from the experiences they are about to undergo.

I remember during a regression session, seeing my wife to be and my doorkeeper guide accompanying me to the Earth plane to be placed into my mother's womb. My wife was eight years younger than I, but my life's experiences with women put me off women until such time as it was right for Linda and me to get together.

Some will become close friends or even lovers; some will cause you problems and distress. My first girlfriend, with whom I was very much in love, caused me as much, if not more, distress than happiness. In the fourteen months that we went out together, she "packed me up" (as we said then), at least six times. I know that she went out with others in that time and one was a married man more than twice her age. This experience made me vow never to be treated like that again and I'm afraid my poor wife suffered because of it. I kept my distance from girls after that even though I was very attracted to several in the ensuing years.

It seems that in this particular life, my experiences are very much being on the receiving end of unhappiness in love because all of the relationships I have had, have had a sting in the tail.

Then, having decided upon the aims and objectives and the people who are going to help you achieve them, (it's a two way process, of course), it has to be decided upon as to which situations best serve this purpose, and so certain gifts are bestowed upon you. Such things as: language skills, aptitude for figure work or maths, music, skills of the artisan, healing, clairvoyance and a multitude of skills which make us the social creatures that we are.

Opportunities are set up to use the aforementioned skills and to come into contact with the people who are to share your life's journey: at work, at clubs, associations of all sorts or sometimes, just a "chance" meeting.

In my own case, (when I was 9 years old) I was moving chairs from the choir gallery, (after the Nativity play), at St.Bartholomews church when I met Henry Madle, the organist and choirmaster. He gave me an audition for the choir on the spot. This was the start of my singing career, because I have been a singer ever since. It was years after joining the choir, that the interest in music engendered by singing in the choir, reaped dividends.

My wife and I became students at the local College of Education when I was mid-thirties, and she, late twenties. We began as History students but, because we spent so much time in the music department doing extra-curricula activities, we were offered places as music students. We jumped at the chance although we weren't really qualified for it; Linda had an 'O' level in Music but all I had was the ability to sing and play the recorder. I became a music teacher but my real interest was in composition. In 1993, my first Mass was performed at St. Bartholomews, where it all began.

Aims and objectives are all concerned with making us better people: to improve our strength of character or, to put it another way, to help us to advance spiritually. Experiences help us to learn such things as how to be more patient, more tolerant, more caring etc.

Seeing the plight of others can make us desire strongly to ease their lot. There are many cases of parents getting involved in or setting up associations to help children because they themselves have lost a child through a particular disease or accident. This also applies to doctors, nurses etc who have been touched by their experiences prior to their desire to help others by using their medical skills.

Frequently, our life's experiences make us stronger in mind and emotionally, as things happen to us or to our loved ones. Losing a loved one is one of the hardest things to come to terms with: to pick up and to enter into everyday life again. Even to have other relationships. I know this from personal experience. When my wife died, I was devastated; particularly because we had both been healing for nearly twenty years and it called into question all that we believed in. It took me a year to start back healing but I was back in circle three weeks after the funeral. For a while, my clairvoyance was brilliant and then went back to normal. It was probably that the shock of losing my wife had opened-up my psychic centres for a while.

As for the healing, I went through a process of great doubt as to whether healing worked, or whether, in fact, that it did work but that I wasn't a particularly good healer. I went through the gamut of emotions and finally, because, I feel, that healing is what I am all about, I went back to join the healing group.

Here, I was further frustrated by the good results that I was getting and I began to ask my guides; "Why can I heal others and not myself or my wife"? It is strange to note that a lot of healers have health problems. They are subject to the laws of the material plain and cannot afford to neglect their health any more than non-healers. I think that it goes further than that. I think that it is a test of whether one is prepared to go on healing others when one's own health is not so good. There must be a lot more "Brownie points" if you continue to help others whilst you yourself are undergoing problems.

So, all these things which are sent to try us have been set out in the contract to which we agreed before coming down to the Earth-plane. We have to soldier on and try to do our best. It is how we react to, and deal with our problems, which indicates our strength of character.

Such experiences, we are told, are supposed to make us stronger. As someone who has lost a very loved wife, I immediately took-up life again. This is not to say that I didn't have times on my own where I sobbed out my grief, but I knew that despite her physical presence being absent, we have never been parted in spirit.

I have also been taught that at each denser level of the spirit realms we acquire another etheric body to enable us to exist at that level. If a spirit from a higher level descends through the spheres to the material plane, by the time of arrival he or she would be encased in several etheric layers making it a not very pleasant experience until they have acclimatised. It's similar to a deep-sea diver where the suit has to withstand greater and greater pressure as the descent is made.

I remember on one of my astral travels arriving back at my body, looking down on it and thinking, "I don't want to get back in there". I remained gazing at my inert body for sometime before I was unceremoniously pushed back into my earthly case. I lay awake for over an hour feeling the unpleasantness of being in a physical body. It felt damp and clammy. Fortunately, I fell asleep and awoke acclimatised to my earthly existence.

It has to be said, however, that there are many born into this life whose sole purpose is to serve others. As well as healers, mediums etc, there are doctors, nurses, and those who care for others in a variety of situations and ways. There are also those scientists who strive to improve our lives through their inventions. This does not mean that they will be free from the usual sort of problems, which we all get. Others will serve by giving guidance to people on their spiritual pathway.


EARTHLY AGE

During my present incarnation I have striven to remain as childlike as possible. This is totally different from being childish. Being childlike is much more fun that the prescribed, "Act your age" which is frequently uttered in our, oh so serious society.

As I write this, I am looking forward to going rock climbing again; at the age of seventy-six. All the people I know who go rock climbing are young at heart.

It's not only that I go rock-climbing. In my seventies, I am apt to walk along walls just like Compo in "Last of the Summer Wine". Of course, I don't get into the scrapes that he did, but I do my best.

The spirit is eternal; therefore, we cannot grow old. Age is a concept of earthly society. How often have you heard the phrase from an elderly person; "I don't feel any different from when I was young"? Too many people decide that, by the time they are about forty, their active live is over. Life will then consist of work and going home to watch television. Often, their gait and demeanour is that of an old person. Such people are usually those who have not had many lives on Earth before. With the right encouragement, they could enhance their lives by refusing to accept the social mores, which tell them to 'Act their age'.


## PHILOSOPHY

I first became interested in philosophy when I was in my teenage years. I loved reading the ancient Greek philosophers. I think it was more for the convoluted dialogues than the actual philosophy, which was hard to determine in the twists and turns of the language. As someone who loves delving into the use, and misuse, of language, I'm sure that those ancient philosophers also had a love and feeling for language.

There can be variations of belief in the Spiritualist movement. Most Spiritualists come from a Christian background, so we have a 'half-way house' as it were, in the Christian Spiritualist movement. There are also, Jews, Muslims and Buddhists in the movement. In fact, mostly, Spiritualists are very tolerant of other religions.

The central philosophy of Christianity is the collections of the 'Sayings of Jesus' and Christians believe that they are solely Christian in origin. If they were to dig a little deeper, they would discover that these sayings were already extant in the Middle East through "The Teacher of Righteousness", who appears in the 'Dead Sea Scrolls. This teacher was a member of the Essenes: an arm of the Jewish faith. According to my researches on the web, the concept of the teacher of righteousness goes back even further to pre-Judean religions. Therefore, it seems to me that philosophy becomes enshrined in religion and not vice versa.

For example, rules and social mores are designed for the good of a tribal or racial group. Basically, the important ones are much the same for all groups. It is important, for a group to survive, that harmony exists in the group, so, monogamy has been important in keeping people from murdering each other for coveting someone else's spouse. Stealing from a member of the group can also lead to friction with dire consequences. I'm sure you get the picture. Should you not; read the Ten Commandments or its equivalent in other religions. These civic regulations have become enshrined in religions, which threaten dire consequences after death. Other, less serious, restraints upon members of groups are due to local circumstances: particularly, climate.

Some major restraints are due to a small group exercising their power and not wishing to lose it: as in the Hindu Caste System.

Reincarnation was an early Christian belief. It is said that, because the lowest members of society often committed suicide to escape their terrible life, to be born at a later date when they might have a much better life, the belief in reincarnation was expunged from the religion and suicide was deemed to be a sin with all the dreadful consequences to be experienced in the afterlife.

Spiritualists know this belief in the dire consequences of suicide to be erroneous. I have often been present when a medium has brought through somebody who committed suicide and they all bring news of having settled in nicely with other members of the family gone before.

They all express regret for the effect, which their suicide has had on their loved ones left behind on Earth.


## SPIRITUALIST PHILOSOPHY

Ask any Spiritualist why it is necessary for us to come to the material plane, and the answer will come back quick as a flash, "To learn lessons".

It seems that people are either simple or need simplistic answers to questions about Life. Life is never simple, and the spiritual journey on Earth is even more convoluted and torturous than the life of someone perceived to be 'not yet on the spiritual pathway. My own belief is that, if you are on the Earth plane, then, you are on the spiritual pathway.

However, all this begs the question of why it is necessary for a spirit, dwelling in the spirit realms, to develop themselves by entering a physical body on the material plane. It occurs to me that this is like saying to a fish, "Go out onto dry land and learn your lessons". If we are Spirit first and foremost, why is it necessary for us to live in an alien environment in order to learn all that we already know before we come to the material plane.

We are not here to learn that we are eternal beings and that the spirit does not die on the death of the physical body. We know that we are eternal beings before we come to the earth-plane. All the knowledge that has ever been, is and shall be is contained in the Spirit World. The Halls of Knowledge are vast beyond our comprehension. If we want to know anything of worth, we can go to these halls to gain it; we do not have to be born into the material world to learn it.

There are many reasons why we come down to Earth.

If we start with the 'lessons' scenario', what do we mean by 'lessons'. They are not like the subject lessons we have in our schools: History, Geography etc. as some people believe. For example, some people believe that we are here to learn that there is life after death, that mediums can 'speak to the dead' etc. Spirit know what they are before they come to the material plane, they don't need to re-learn it on Earth. The lessons are to do with, how to deal with life and with our fellow travellers. We learn not to be unkind to those who are different to us. We learn to be polite, caring, gentle, not to react to people who upset us.

We learn to be strong in situations where strength is needed. We learn endurance, perseverance; we learn to be serious minded but carefree and gay.

These become our character traits, so, the purpose is that of building strength of character and gentleness of nature.

Therefore, the reason, in this case, of coming down to the material plane is for character building. I feel that my own life has been much the same as that of a young man in a primitive culture being sent out into the wilderness to face known and unknown dangers and to triumph over them. My entire life has been fraught with emotional stress through a whole variety of agencies.

If a person finds life too difficult to cope, and commits suicide, they are not punished when they arrive in the spirit world for, it is punishment enough for them not to have achieved the goals which they set out to achieve when they came to the material world. They review their life and perhaps will set out to make amends to those whom were left behind.

The reason for their suicide was that their earthly mind over-rode their spiritual mind and they were unable to see any other way out of their situation. On arrival in Spirit, the spiritual mind is able to function without hindrance from the earthly mind and they can see things more clearly.

Another reason for coming to the Earth is to help others, not just in a material way, but to help develop their spirituality.

Mediums and healers do just this. Many people who are healed either through hands on healing, or through messages received through mediums, decide that they too would like to help others, and so set off on their own spiritual pathway. The spirit coming to Earth for a brief moment of time comes into this category for the reasons already given in chapter one.

My mother was the sort of person that all members of the family who needed help, went to my mother to get it. She was always there and never stinted on the help that she gave. When a work colleague was homeless, she became our lodger for a while. Whenever there was bereavement in the family, everyone gathered at our house. It was my mother who set me off on my spiritual journey by taking me, and my wife to a clairvoyant meeting. This reason comes under the category of 'Service'. That is to God and to Man.

However, I believe that the prime reason for coming to the material plane is to refine our spiritual being: to increase our vibratory rate and thus be able to ascend to higher realms. The Spiritualist principle: Eternal progress open to every human soul, tells us that we never stop improving ourselves. Many philosophies believe that we begin as an intrinsic part of the Godhead and then refine ourselves until we are fit to rejoin the source of all being.

It is very sad that many people get bogged down in the philosophy of their religion. When I was a teenager. I had many friends in the Presbyterian Church. One of their sayings that made an impression on me, was, "If someone gets a good idea that will benefit Mankind, the Devil will change it into a religion.

One of my favourite books is the collection of short stories by Giovanni Guareschi, based on the antics of a parish priest called Don Camillo. One of the passages in this book struck a chord with me. It concerns a parable told to Don Camillo.

A hundred men were in a dark room where nobody could see anyone else. Each man had a lamp, which was not burning. One man found a way to light his lamp so that the people nearest to him could see their own lamps and could, therefore, light them. Gradually, the whole room was filled with light, as more and more lamps became lit. Then, some men began to worship their own lamp as the one true lamp and they neglected their lamps as they spent time bowing down to their lamp in worship. Gradually, the room darkened as each lamp in turn went out. This, to me, is a perfect analogy of religion. Together, the men were able to see the whole truth. By focusing on their own particular piece of truth, they were plunged into the darkness of ignorance once again.

The seven Principles of Spiritualism were conceived when, if people weren't particularly Christian, Christianity was the predominant philosophy in the Western world. Thus, I feel, a certain obeisance was paid to that fact when the principles were set up. (Originally given by the spirit of the philanthropist, Robert Owen).

Thus we have: The fatherhood of God, the brotherhood of Man, the ministry of Angels and the communion of Spirits.

These are the first three principles and show a distinct alignment with the Christian religion.

The Spiritualist National Union have realized that these wordings are not appropriate to modern thinking but, instead of changing the wording of the principles to reflect what they do believe in, they have issued a book, "Philosophy of Spiritualism" in which the 'Fatherhood of God becomes very much expanded to include, 'Motherhood' and going so far as the accept the fact that God is something beyond the comprehension of Mankind. Something I was aware of long before the book was issued.

The 'Brotherhood of Man' becomes extended, not only to women, but also to all creatures of the Earth.

The book is well worth reading and, I feel, that the philosophy is very appropriate to present day living.

Spiritualists all seem to agree that the most important principle is: "Personal Responsibility". (I think the most important principle is: "The continuous existence of the human soul, because everything stems from that). Whereas

Christians go to a priest to be absolved, Spiritualist know that we must accept our own blame and, when we go to Spirit, we must face our misdeeds committed on Earth. This is accompanied by the knowledge that we are not punished, (as priests would have it), but, as part of our spiritual growth, we make amends at some future date.

The one principle, I find, that is incongruous is "Compensation and retribution for all the good and evil deeds done on Earth". This doesn't really fit in with the belief that we are not punished for our misdeeds but rather we are faced with them when we go over, and we decide what to do about it. We might accept that we have to make recompense in some way or we might believe that we were in the right; that the way we treated somebody whilst on Earth, was right for that situation. We might even think that it was beneficial for their spiritual development.

What I cannot accept is something that I heard a well- known teacher, (not a Spiritualist), say. She said that before we come to the Earth-plane, another spirit, out of love, will come to the Earth to be cruel, nasty etc. to us in order for us to spiritually grow. I'm sure such situations arise because the antagonist is naturally cruel or nasty. We can volunteer to be put into that situation for our spiritual growth but that is it.

We are all on individual journeys. When we first come to the Earth Plane, we are not interested in religion. We are more interested in experiencing the delights, which are on offer.

After several such lifetimes, we begin to think that there is something more to life and this is when religion becomes important in our lives. Religion is a necessary stage through which we go.

After several lifetimes attached to a particular religion, we move on to experience another religion. We have to experience them all before we get to the stage where no religion seems appropriate to our needs. We seek to become spiritual without the restraints of religion.

It is not a race; we all start at A and finish at B. There is no need to hurry; we have eternity in which to develop.

# RE-INCARNATION

I have deliberately used the heading in this way because it shows more clearly the fact that we are born many times into this life. It must be said, here, that reincarnation is not part of the Spiritualist religion, although many individuals in the movement, do believe in it.

We all know someone who is either a 'first timer' or who has had only a few incarnations. These people are more concerned with the pleasures of life than in caring for others. Indeed, many of them believe that misfortunes such as being out of work or being unable to pay medical bills etc. is down to profligacy or inherent idleness. Such was the philosophy of many Victorians who believed that worthy people would never be in such positions. The philosophy of "Self-help" was a keystone in this philosophy. If you fell on hard times, it was your own fault; not the fault of greedy landowners or mill owners or any of their ilk. Unfortunately, this philosophy has not entirely died out.

The more incarnations we have, the more we become aware of and concerned for others.

Again, there are those who believe in numbers and I have heard various opinions as to how many lives we have on the earth plane. Again, the clue is in the word, "eternal", and in the Spiritualist Principles, "Eternal progress open to every human soul" shows how fallacious it is to put limits on everything.

My guides have told me that I have had in the region of 10,000 lives on the Earth. When you consider that Man has been on the Earth for more years than scientists have yet discovered, then this can begin to make sense.

Other factors make this clearer. It is said that Mankind first appeared in North Africa and spread out from there. It is also said that there were only a few thousand of these beings. If we consider that there are now around 6 billion (the new, English, billion) people on Earth, then we must consider that there have been a lot of generations since the beginning.

Moreover, life expectancy was very much shorter than it is now. It is only since the 18th. Century that hygiene, food supply, medication etc. that we have gained the longer life span that people enjoy now. There were also many premature deaths due to disease, tribal warfare etc.

Until the introduction of the Edinburgh, "Lying-in" hospitals, mother and baby fatalities were very high.

Even some of the English royal families had very high mortality rates among their children. Queen Anne is said to have had 18 children all who died.

We must also remember that civilizations arise and then die out. We know of stories about the Atlantians. Who knows how many times mankind has appeared on Earth and then died out for one reason or another? If this is so, then, mankind could have been roaming the Earth plane millions of years ago, not just the 30/40 thousand years which scientists now claim.

So if we take the average life span into account, there is ample opportunity for us to have had many, many previous lives. That is why we shouldn't get hung up upon one.

We are all high born, low born and in between, in one incarnation or another. It is nice to know about previous incarnations but we are here to live this one.

## FATALISM

So many people believe that everything that happens is pre-ordained. When my wife died, I lost count of how many people said, "It was meant to be." Or "It was her time to go". While I can accept that many things are "meant to be", we live in a world of limitless possibilities. Fatalism was a characteristic of Eastern religions, which was scorned in the West, but now seems to be gaining ground among, at least, the British.

It is my opinion that we are given guidelines of the life-to-be before we incarnate; not blueprints. So, we are given things to achieve, goals to reach, etc. but, as stated previously, if we do not achieve our targets, then, there are incarnations before us in which we can achieve our goals. Nothing is set in stone. Moreover, we can go beyond that which has been set for us. Once we have reached our goals, we can achieve even greater things than we had hoped for before we came to the Earth plane.

Nothing is set in stone: accidents can happen that were not foreseen. When I was young, I was pushed, by another boy, towards a drop of about two hundred feet. My life might have ended then, and you wouldn't be reading this. I'm sure that people would have told my parents, "It was meant to be." The fact that I am writing this book will cause others to say, "It was meant to be." I was actually saved from making the drop by another friend, who grabbed me as I was near the edge.

If we think that simply everything is meant to be, we are no more than automatons, or puppets. If I use the analogy of the 'Rite of passage", then it is perhaps easier to see that we are plunged into a world where anything can happen, and not just that which we planned.

## KARMA

When I worked regularly in a healing clinic, from time to time people would come for healing believing that all their problems had come about because of their behaviour in a previous life. They had caused pain, in some form or other, and now they were being punished for it.

Nothing is further from the truth. If they were to study the religions from which the idea of Karma comes, they would discover that Karma is merely a continuation of the learning process in the material world. Of course, Buddhists and Hindus would talk about cause and effect but the important thing to remember is that there is no punishment. It is not the same as the Catholic view, which does preach punishment for misdeeds, (or sins).

I think it is best to view karma as simply the ongoing process of continuous learning for the spirit.

We had to convince people that they could overcome their problems; that if they forgot about their, "karmic doom", their lives and health could improve. By thinking that their problems were due to karma, they told themselves that it was a punishment and there was nothing they could do about it.

The main thing to remember is, there is always something that can be done to improve situations. The Spiritualist principal no 7 is: Eternal progress open to every human soul. This is the proper way to regard Karma.

# CHAPTER FOUR

## RELIGION AND SPIRITUALITY

My mother was always saying, "You don't have to go to church to be a Christian" When I grew older, I used to say, "Yes you do, that's what Christians do. It's like a club. If you belong to a club, you have to abide by the rules of the club and attend meetings and functions". It was more difficult in those days to differentiate between Religion and Spirituality because there was not the information about that there is today. Being a member of a religion does not preclude people from being spiritual but often they are kept in separate boxes. Many people used to say, "You shouldn't mix religion with politics". I would disagree. If your religion is at odds with your politics, to be consistent, you must change one or the other. I had an argument about this with my father-in-law after Mass; one Sunday lunchtime. He started on about the young priest who had taken the service that morning. To cut a long story short, I said to him, "If your religion tells you to share all you have with your fellow man but your politics tells you, everyman for himself and blow those less fortunate than yourself, you cannot abide by both those precepts, you shouldn't compartmentalise". It is our ability to compartmentalise that gives rise to such tensions in our thinking.

If a person is religious, then they will follow the customs of their religion. If they are Catholic they will attend Mass, make the sign of the cross on their forehead with holy water as they enter they church, they will stand-up, sit-down at the appropriate times and join in the prayers and responses as indicated. They will believe in infant baptism and a dogma set down by the church.

So, Religion is conforming to a set behaviour pattern laid down by priests, ministers etc. Spirituality is living life in a way that takes into consideration, the needs of others. To be "caring and sharing" if you like. There are many people like this, some of whom attend conformist churches and others who don't. Some people profess to be atheist but live spiritual lives and some are more spiritual than people who attend a church every week. I worked for a man once who told me that he went to church only to meet business colleagues after the service rather than going to church for altruistic reasons. In fact, he wasn't particularly enamoured of religion.

# CHAPTER FIVE

## CLAIRVOYANCE

Clairvoyance is a generic term covering, clairvoyance, clair-audience, clair-sensing, pyschic aura reading and esp.

Clairvoyance means "Clear seeing" it can be broken down into two branches: seeing Spirit and Seeing symbols or pictures. The latter is usually received from spirit guides. A lot of mediums use this method and some of them don't realise it. For example, symbolically, a house represents the person receiving a message from the medium. If the medium sees a house on fire, this means that the person is going through a cleansing process, not that their house is going to burn down. A friend of mine was worried for weeks when she was given this symbol.

Symbols can also be picked-up psychically from the aura. A lot of information can be given in a symbol whether received from spirit or from the aura. I like to use symbols as an adjunct to clairvoyance. In one picture, an awful lot of information is contained.

Clair-audience is the ability to hear spirit, but this can occur in different ways.

Highly developed mediums can hear the voice of the spirit relaying the message; others might hear their own voice or just get thoughts put into their minds. All of these are degrees of clair-audience and sometimes mediums get a mixture of them all.

Clair-sensing is where a medium gets "feelings". This can be physical impressions such as feeling sick or getting a specific kind of pain in an area, (to demonstrate evidence of the spirit communicator), or emotional feelings such as sadness, apprehension, joy and the like. It can also tell you if they were generous, outgoing or introvert, sporty or bookish etc. Some people consider this to be the best form of mediumship because it can bring the communicator very close in the mind of the recipient.

Some people are psychics rather than mediums. A medium is specifically someone who can see and/or hear Spirit. Psychics can link into earth energies to give healing and/or link into people's auras to pick-up information stored there.

This is usually information regarding present or past events but sometimes can refer to the future. In skilled hands, this type of reading can be quite accurate but often it is inadequate.

ESP is mind to mind reading and is very rare. In our training circles, we used to do exercises to develop this skill. One of the sitters would think of a shape; square, circle or triangle, and would try to keep the shape in mind whilst the other sitters would try to link in to find out what shape was being transmitted.

This would also be done with colours, red, green and blue, and then we would progress to a coloured shape.

To develop mediumship, it is ideal to sit in an established circle with an experienced medium. The medium must know how to control the circle and be able to maintain discipline. They must also be able to develop each sitter's individual talents. Too many circles are run to the lines on which the medium, their self was developed. There must be room for people to develop their individual gifts; such as those listed above. My wife and I sat in a circle with a very good medium but he came out of circle as quite a young man and didn't bother to develop himself thereafter. Linda and I knew a lot more than he did and he got a bit fed-up with us after a while, and we were with him for only a couple of months.

Some mediums have been disciplined enough to develop their gift by sitting on their own at home. One very good medium I saw at a local church told us that he sat for seven years on his own. That is dedication to the art.

People attending meetings for the first time can be forgiven for being confused when they hear the medium "giving-off". There is a tendency to use the same language to mean different things. The most common phrases are, "They are telling me", or "Spirit are telling me". One would think that this meant that the medium was hearing a voice but it doesn't very often mean that. I have been to workshops where students have been told to use these terms instead of, "I'm seeing such and such" or "I feel that", etc.

If the medium can hear Spirit, it is most likely that the message is true, (taking into account that people do not change when they go into Spirit, so if the medium doesn't use their guide and lets any spirit person communicate the verity of the message can be open to doubt).

However, if the demonstrator is merely seeing or getting impressions, then this might come from Spirit or they might be picking-up impressions from the aura, on to which they might apply erroneous interpretations.

Good mediums will give evidence about just one or two people in Spirit. Beware of the medium, (and I have heard it many times), who will say just one thing about a host of people: " You know somebody who died of a heart-attack; you knew a man who smoked a pipe; you know somebody who died before their time etc" My favourite is the one given by a very popular local medium: "You knew somebody who left a ring behind." Of course they did; they can't take it with them. Everybody who ever died went to Spirit taking none of their earthly possessions with them. Most people can remember all of those things relating to different people in their lives. This is not evidence at all; it's more like 'trawling' "Mediums" who work like this usually work on a psychic level and give psychic messages; which is probably why they are popular with some people.

Good evidence paints a convincing picture of the communicator: It will include several items about the same person. "I have a lady here giving the name of Jane, who died of a heart-attack when she was 63, (or early 60s). She was a professional lady who worked as an administrator." Etc.

The most important part of mediumship is to bring the essence of the communicator through to the recipient, so that the recipient can almost feel the physical presence of their loved one. This is, indeed, possible and has been proved to be so on many occasions. I, myself, love this communication when it happens through my mediumship. This is clair-sentience at its best.

It is difficult for mediums to know the meaning of everything that they see but, all too often they interpret something without giving-off what they have seen. For example, they might be shown a boat on a stormy sea and interpret this as meaning that the recipient is going through a difficult time, (Sea of Life being stormy). If they had just said what they had seen, the person might recollect that they were indeed in a boat during a storm. The reverse also applies; the medium might have said something like, "Did you ever go out in a boat when the sea was stormy"? If not, then the symbology would apply. It is worth noting that symbols can mean different things to different medium; this is particularly true in respect of colours.

I was at a gathering of healers taking part in a healing meditation lead by Betty Shine. She talked us through the meditation using the colour "Blue". At the end of the meditation, one lady said she couldn't follow the meditation because she always used "White" for healing. I wouldn't say that this was a genuine complaint but you can see the problem.

We were always taught that the basic healing colour was green, (as in Nature); blue was for calming and that white contained all the other colours within it and could be used in any circumstance.

I always tell people who ask about cleaning chakras to visualise white light because, not only is this cleansing, but each chakra will take the colour it needs from it. Colour is only a perception in the mind and people do perceive things differently so, I think, it is wrong for mediums to specify a particular meaning to a recipient. They should just give the interpretation. It will make a difference, of course as to where the colour is situated. There are many layers to the aura and it surely depends on the layer or chakra in which the colour is perceived.

Often, mediums talk as though they can see your entire aura. This is very seldom true; what they can normally see, is a particular colour which is relevant to what is going-on in the life of the person at that moment of time.

I would like to mention my own pet hate at this juncture; mediums who do not use their guides when giving clairvoyance. The result is often a rambling, incoherent message with the medium giving-off names of friends and relatives who are shouting them out from spirit. I always ask my guides to direct my mediumship. I ask them to give me specific information, which will enable me to find the recipient quickly. I have been able to do this with just two or three pieces of specific information. In one case, with just one piece of evidence, which was the name of a village in which the communicator was born. I did not know that such a village existed, as it was about two hundred miles away. On another occasion, I found the recipient with the name of the communicator and the country in which they were born. Both the name and the country were unusual. Names are not evidence unless accompanied by good information about the communicator.

Often, the medium is unable to leave a recipient because the communicator from Spirit, "Won't let me go". My teacher, when on the platform, always worked with her guide. He would organise the spirit people and tell them to choose a spokes-person to give the message. The result was a short but meaningful message with regards sent from the people who were waiting in the background but not allowed to chip in.

I think that five minutes is ample to give evidence and a message; ten minutes at the most to make it more interesting. I knew a young medium who used to give short but evidential messages; he would give everyone three to four minutes but it was all good; evidential and with a message.

When I first attended Spiritualist meetings with my wife, (my mother took us), all mediums would go direct to a person: "I would like to come to the lady in the green cardigan", was the sort of thing that they would say. Many mediums, however, give-off evidence and rely on people in the audience to speak up if the evidence is recognised. Many of the best mediums work in this way but there are mediums who give-off the weakest of evidence and then ask who the message is for:

"I have a lady here who never went out without her handbag" is the sort of thing that I've heard. Then instead of getting more solid evidence, they pitch in with, "can anyone accept that".

I feel like yelling, "Of course we can, we all can". The result of this type of clairvoyance is often, what has become known as, 'Split messages'. After two or three bits of this type of vague evidence, two or three people try to claim the message and, often, two or three people get bits of information which one or the other of them can accept. Sceptical psychologists would have a field day observing this type of "clairvoyance". I was at a demonstration where the medium went to three people before finally getting to the right person on the fourth go.

She then gave some evidence, which I accepted, but she thought that she was with the "gentleman in the back row". (I was in the front row). For five minutes she tried to give the message to the man at the back who could accept nothing of which she said. Finally, she said to me, "I think I'm with you, dear, unfortunately, I haven't time to give you a message". I could have strangled her. On other occasions, I have been present when a medium has given a message to three people at the same time, "Which of you knows a man who used to smoke a pipe"? "Who can accept someone with a knee injury"? This sort of mediumship is a disgrace to the world of spirit.

A well known, very good, psychic artist, Ivor James, used to say, "I will give four pieces of evidence to go with the drawing; you must accept all four pieces".

Sure enough, people would be putting up their hands and saying, "I can accept two/three pieces of the evidence", but Ivor would insist on the four. I received a drawing of my grandmother from him after accepting the four bits of evidence.

Another problem which occurs with mediums not using their guides, is the fact that, once a person has spoken-up to accept part of the evidence, their loved ones from the other side latch- on to their vibration and jump in, perhaps pushing out of the way some spirit whose loved one was more judicious in accepting the evidence. Therefore, the person who should have got the message can lose out.

Having said all that, if the quality of evidence is good, then this style of mediumship is equally, if not more, valid. If the medium can find the recipient with just a few pieces of solid evidence, then this is really good mediumship. For example: "I have a lady here who tells me her name is Rose, she lived to her mid eighties and lived in a terraced house numbered 36".

So, you have to be on your toes when participating in a clairvoyant demonstration. It takes time, but you learn to discriminate between various qualities of mediumship.

Never be afraid to speak-up if you think that the evidence the medium is giving-off is for you. It does happen occasionally that a medium misplaces a message. Some mediums will speak about this before they begin the demonstration and ask people to speak-up if the person receiving the message can't accept it and someone else can.

Many a time, I have heard a medium give a message such as: "By next Spring, the problems you are experiencing will have been resolved." or "This time next year your health will be much better and you will be filled with vitality." When such prophecies fail to come true or take somewhat longer to materialise, the stock phrase is, "Well, my dear, you know there is no such thing as Time in Spirit." To which I feel like yelling, "Well, why did you say it in the first place?"

If Spirit do give a time, it is obvious that they do know when something should happen. Not everything that we plan happens and not everything that should happen does happen. Partly, because we have free-will, but also because accidents happen. In fact, there is no such thing as Time on the Earth-plane: Mankind has got together to agree upon a scale of events called Time.

This is arbitrary. Some civilisations based their time on the Moon, others on the seasons etc. Present-day time is based on the rotation of the Earth and its orbit of the sun.

So don't accept time as given by mediums as a fact, but take the essence of what they say and believe that it will happen.

Like everything else in life, there are some good mediums, some mediocre mediums and some who shouldn't be on the platform. Also, remember that everybody has good days and bad days so never write-off a medium on one performance; give them chance to prove themselves, particularly if they are new to the platform: it is a terrifying experience which takes a lot of getting used to. It can take quite a long time for a medium who has proved themselves in circle to settle in to platform demonstrations.


## PSYCHOMETRY

Psychometry is, properly, the reading of the vibrations of an object. It is, therefore, a reading about the object rather than its wearer or owner; such things as, e.g., where it came from, the processes it was subjected to in the making of it etc. Anything else, strictly speaking, is some form of clairvoyance. If one begins to pick-up spirit people through Psychometry, it has moved on to mediumship,

The medium of one circle in which I sat was very keen on psychometry because, he said, it was a lead-in to proper mediumship. His method of reading objects was quite novel, although he had been taught it by another medium. Any object could be read; e.g. the number of keys in a bunch could relate to the number of people in a family. One large key would represent the dominant member of the family; two large keys could represent a balanced partnership etc. If an object was broken, this could represent a broken partnership. It was always amazing to us students how accurate this appeared to be.

Moving-on from eye-observation, we were then asked to give-off our feelings about the object. We could then gather the emotional state of the owner of the object. This is clair-sentience.

Strictly speaking, Psychometry, is the reading of the vibrations on an object. As it often leads on to clairvoyance or clair-sensing, it is often confusing to people as to what it is. I remember going to Boundary Passage Spiritualist church in the early1980s and looking at the notices board to see that Psychometry had been crossed out. I asked the president, Florrie Jemi why this was and was told that someone had complained under the Trades Descriptions act that they had been given clairvoyance and not psychometry.

## TRANCE MEDIUMSHIP

The trance state covers a wide range of what is commonly known by practitioners of the art as "Altered State of Consciousness". This is because they have to lower the rate of their brain wave vibrations in order for a spirit to merge their mind with them.

When I do trance healing, I prefer to call it "Attunement healing".

Traditionally, there are four basic levels of consciousness: Beta, Alpha, Theta and Delta.

The Beta state is when you are consciously going about your daily tasks, using your brain in an alert state. In tedious, repetitive tasks, it is very easy to drift into the Alpha state, day dreaming about winning the lottery or about your next holiday and the like. One can reach this state when sitting for relaxation or meditation.

Theta state is a deep meditative state, associated with a much deeper trance state and with the Delta state comes deep, dreamless sleep and unconsciousness. It has recently been discovered that there are deeper states, which can be achieved.

Using various mind techniques, the trance medium can induce the deeper altered states to achieve various types of mediumship. One might liken it to self-hypnosis. Each succeeding depth will achieve a greater level of attunement with Spirit.

It is very rare these days, for any medium to go into deep trance. In fact, the lighter trances might just as well be called "attunement". This is a state where the medium is well aware of where they are and what they are doing. They may also be very aware of Spirit around them. This depth of trance is ideal for healers because, the more in tune with Spirit they are, the better quality of healing they will attain.

## PHYSICAL MEDIUMSHIP

Physical mediumship most usually takes years to develop and takes place in circle conditions. The phenomena that take place in these conditions are: Direct voice, Apports and Spirit manifestation. Leslie Flint was, probably, the most famous Direct voice medium.

Direct voice is where spirit voices can be heard by everyone in the room with or without the aid of a specially designed 'trumpet'. I was privileged to hear direct voice on one occasion in my own home. This was only after the energies had built up to such an extent, that I heard my wife's voice clearly saying, "Hello darling". The chances of such a thing happening to anyone are astronomical. Apports are objects that appear in the circle. They can be mundane objects or such things as jewellery or coins etc. With sufficient power and ectoplasm, a spirit can be manifested in its entirety and walk around the circle speaking to sitters and even hugging them. Sometimes, only part of the spirit is manifested; the head or hand, for example.

Transfiguration is also a physical energy art. This is where the medium produces ectoplasm in front of the face and Spirit place their own face in the ectoplasm so that everyone in the room can see the change and loved ones can recognise the spirit. If not everyone can see the spirit face, then it is not transfiguration but, perhaps, overshadowing.

Physical energy healing can remove or dissolve tumours, reset bones and many other miraculous things. It is extremely rare. Harry Edwards is the most well known exponent of this form of healing.

# CHAPTER SIX

## LEYLINES AND EARTH ENERGIES

Leylines are lines of magnetic force radiating from the North Pole to the South Pole.

From these lines, other lines can be created to form a grid-like pattern covering the whole of the Earth. These lines can be tapped into by psychics, healers etc, to bring about, what some people might call "miracles". When practitioners work with the Earth's leylines, spiritual leylines are brought into play to work alongside the magnetic energies of the Earthplane.

As well as leylines, there are local energy centres, (such as stone circles or places of ritual), which can be used as sources for power to bring about 'super-natural' effects. Wherever psychic or spiritual work is carried out, energy centres are created. If the work is only temporary, the energy centre and its attendant leylines will fade away.

The basic, major, leylines are, as has been said, those which radiate out from the North Pole, flowing to the South Pole. The Earth itself is a huge magnet caused by the spin around its axis. The centre of the Earth is a core of iron. The crust spins faster than the core and this is what gives rise to the magnetic field. It can thus be seen that leylines do not just cover the surface of the planet but lie, also, deep within.

Although the lines are magnetic in origin, the pattern on the Earth's surface is not that of a magnetic field. This is because, like electricity, the flow of the line can be attracted to 'nodal' points which might be close by; such things as mineral deposits, forests, rivers, streams etc as well as man-made structures and events such as church rituals or energy patterns caused by repeated actions like meditation, healing or even mundane pursuits such as walking an habitual pathway or working in the shed at the bottom of the garden.

Local energies can be geographical; e.g. due to mineral deposits etc. or such features as lakes, hills, trees etc. These can combine to produce an energy pattern peculiar to the local area. Such features are of interest to the Geomancer or Feng-Shui practitioner. Most leylines are branch lines from branch lines (ad infinitum) of the major leylines.

Nobody can be very far from a line, however minor. This energy system brings life and vibrancy to all things: animal, vegetable and mineral. Occasionally, a leyline can have negative effects. This occurs when there is an imbalance between the positive and negative (yin and yang) energies within the line. Too much of either will result in a 'black line'. Where such a line runs through a house or other building, unpleasant things can occur. The occupants might suffer continued bouts of illness, depression and the like. They might become argumentative or bloody-minded. When the energies of the line are balanced, harmony is restored. Buildings which have negative energies are very often colder than is usual. After re-alignment, the temperature very quickly rises to normal. It is, of course, possible, through the use of Earth acupuncture, to divert the line away from or around the house. In either case, an expert needs to be called-in.

House re-alignment is the correction of energy patterns aligned to the property. All properties have their own basic energy fields. It is when these fields become corrupted by negative influences (violent thoughts or deeds) that disruptive energy patterns can arise (e.g. squares, spirals etc).

Sometimes, of course, the energy patterns were established long before the present building was erected (e.g. site of battlefield, prison or other untoward happenings).

The need for energy-re-alignment is brought to our attention by people complaining of e.g. a constant feeling of being unwell or actually being unwell, feeling tired and drained all the time, irritable or given to moodiness etc.

When this affects the whole family, we know that there is a problem to be investigated. If the problem affects only one member of the family, after discarding more mundane reasons, we might assume that only part of the house, perhaps only one room is involved.

The energy source maintaining the problem is usually coming from a nearby leyline. This is why we look at the map before going to the site, to see what sort of buildings there are in the area. Where there is a very old church, or a new one built on an old site, there is bound to be a leyline, because the first Christian churches were built on pagan sites, and these sites were mostly built on leyline surge-points (pulse-points) where energy is concentrated.

Before going-out to the house, we ensure that we have a form for taking case notes. As we enter the premises, we try to be aware of any sensations, which might be relevant: is the house cold, do we feel comfortable or are we inclined to shiver? Do the occupants seem at ease or otherwise, etc?

Having greeted the occupants, there are questions to be asked of them to help us to find possible causes and/or origins of the problem.

First of all, we ask for a detailed report of the occupants' health. It is very important that we ascertain when the health problems began. They might have begun shortly after moving into the premises, or perhaps when alterations were made to the building.

Sometimes, the problem started soon after some unpleasant neighbours moved in. Also important is the state of health of pets and plants. Sometimes, plants thrive in some positions but wither in others. This, of course, highlights problem areas of the property.

Finding out about the previous occupants can also help. Did they experience similar problems, what sort of people were they? Were they troublesome, violent types or otherwise. Did they have any information about the history of the property or the area, either in the recent past or longer ago?

Having asked all the questions, we then say a prayer in the main room asking for our guides to link closely with us and help us to feel the vibrations; nodal points and energy lines. We then proceed to the room furthest away from the main room to begin our work. The final room to be re-aligned will be the main room, so if there is a cellar, this is done before the main room.

In each room, we dowse the energies to see what shapes, if any, we can find. Shapes like triangles, crescent moons, half-circles, will have nodal points (where the energy is stronger) at the extremities.

Other shapes to be found are, circles, fountains, pentagons, cones, diamond, five pointed/six pointed stars and dimensional doorways; unless the occupier is working with spirit on the premises, these shapes are also dispersed. If you find a triangle in each corner of the room, then this has to be dispersed because it, also, is an opening between dimensions.

In each room, having found the energy patterns, we say a prayer asking that our guides disperse or transform all negative energies and send leyline energy back to the base line. We ask then for a circle of protection to be placed around the room. As we leave each room, the door is closed and blessed with the sign of the cross. This, in effect, asks for a guide to stand on guard at the door so that nothing can re-enter the room.

We also say a prayer and give a blessing in all large walk-in cupboards. The toilet, bathroom and hallways are also included. Usually, the feeder leyline energy is very strong in hallways. To disperse these lines, we form a chain by linking hands with each end person placing a hand on the end wall or door whilst the prayers are being said.

We leave the main living room to the last and when all negative energies have been dispersed, and the leyline energy has been sent to the base line and sealed-off, we say a general prayer for the well being of the house and all occupants. Often, we find that the energies are much weaker here because we have already cut-off the feeder energy lines. If there has been Spirit lingering around the house, if it is not family or friend, our guides take them over into Spirit. There is no question about this. Spirit, belong in the spirit world, and once they are taken there, they would not wish to return to the Earth, except to visit their loved ones.

We then, protect the house by enclosing it in a silver circle containing a golden triangle. It is very important, when dealing with flats, to seal-off from the other occupancies.

Very often, it is noticeable that there is a marked change in the atmosphere of the house even before we have left. Sometimes the occupants themselves notice it. They say that the house feels, calmer, nicer, warmer etc. Frequently, they phone a few days later to tell us that the house has improved and that they themselves feel better.

# CHAPTER SEVEN

## SPIRITS GHOSTS AND POLTERGEISTS

Ghost is a generic term covering several phenomena but, it has to be said, some of them erroneously.

Everybody talks about ghosts: the general public, the media etc. There is not usually any cognizance that they are different phenomena.

Most usually, the reference to a ghost is in respect of the spirit or soul of a departed person. Thus, there are many reports of people seeing the ghost of someone close to them who has recently parted. Properly, what they have seen is a spirit. A spirit is that part of a person which survives earthly death and it has cognizance. Spirits recognise us and are able, through a medium, to communicate with us. They can bring feelings, tastes and aromas with them to help our recognition.

Sometimes, what a person thinks is a spirit, is just an imprint on the ether, (the substance of the Earth-plane). Everything that we say or do is recorded on the ether but sometimes it is recorded so strongly that, under certain conditions, it can be perceived by almost anyone. These conditions are connected to phases of the Moon and to energy shifts in the locality of the phenomena.

The energy supporting this phenomenon is emotion. Persistent actions, such as the patrolling of a section of Hadrian's Wall by a Roman soldier thinking of the warmth of his homeland, could give rise to a strong imprint on the Ether. One house-realignment that we did, featured a woman waking the man of the house at five am every day with a cup of tea. This was at a fisherman's cottage in Portslade where the woman, in times gone by, used to wake-up her husband in the same fashion. This repeated action was intense enough to be strongly recorded and thence put into play like a video playback.

Violent action can also give rise to ghosts. Here, the emotion is really intense. Murder, torture and the like, engender fear and pain and, sometimes, the scenes are played-out time and time again according to the prevailing energy conditions.

Sometimes, demolishing a wall can release its ghosts. That is why we always ask on a call-out, whether there have been any alterations carried out.

Ghosts, being merely an energy imprint, are not cognizant. They just exist having no recognition or ability other than to carry-out the same action over and over again.

Spirit can "haunt" the Earth-plane for a variety of reasons.

One house we went to on the outskirts of Lewes, was in an area where witches had been burned or otherwise executed. The house was being haunted by quite a number of spirits and odd things were going on to upset the householders. Our client told someone she knew living in the area that we were going to exorcise her spirits and put her house energies right. This woman claimed to be a witch and said that she would stop us carrying it out. On the way there, we had three very near miss accidents in the car but we got there alright; our guides were stronger than her spells. The energies in the house were such as to allow free access to any spirit to come in at any time. The sitting room was completely wide open as an access point. Normally, Spirit, enter via what we call a "Dimensional Door", but this was the whole area of the room. We have found this in one or two other places.

In the fisherman's cottage, mentioned earlier, the lady of the house was being upset by a spirit blowing cigarette smoke into her face. This turned-out to be the previous wife of the husband who was obviously annoyed with the woman for taking her place. When the guides had taken the spirit across to the other side and we had sealed all dimensional doors, the Alsatian dog went across to where the door had been and started whining. The spirit had been his only company during the day when its owners were out to work.

Poltergeists are often referred to as ghosts. They exist in two distinct and unrelated forms. Firstly, the effects of things being thrown around a room or weird noises, can be entirely due to kinetic energy generated by pubescent teenagers; usually, girls. This energy is given-off violently through the histrionic emotional feelings of the child. This is why we always ask if there are any teenagers in the house when responding to poltergeist activity.

The other form of poltergeist activity is brought about by very low level discarnate beings attracted to the house either by the dark thoughts of a member of the household or by uncontrolled Ouija-board practises and the like. These beings live off of the fear, which they create. Sending them loving thoughts will encourage them to depart.

Sometimes, what people regard as poltergeist activity is merely the result of a loved one in Spirit, trying to attract their attention; to let them know that they are still alive and well and also to let them know that they are still connected by the love which exists between them.

One house we went to exhibited photos and other objects being moved. Unfortunately, a picture frame fell to the floor, breaking the glass. We were called in and I became aware of a gentleman. I described him and the lady shouted out, "I'll kill him". It was her husband whom I had described.

# CHAPTER EIGHT

## HEALING

The word 'Heal' is a very complex word. It has root associations with the word 'Whole' and can also be linked to the word 'well'. The words, 'Health' and 'Wealth' also have connections. 'Alternative' practitioners like to stress that they concentrate on the 'Whole' person' and that they strive to make people well and whole again. Some people say that 'health is all the wealth that you need'. As you can imagine, such a complex word gives rise to a complex array of ideas as to what 'healing' is or does.

There are, therefore, many, many types of healing and approaches to healing. I do believe that doctors and nurses of the orthodox medical approach can be classed as 'Healers'. Their approach to healing might not be in line with the general ideas of healing, but there is no denying that they have an important role in saving lives and helping people to recover from disease. Having said that, many of the orthodox treatments cause unpleasant side-effects and can lead, if not controlled properly, to unnecessary complications. It is good to see that orthodox medical practitioners are beginning to embrace some of the alternative therapies, which, therefore, are also called 'complementary' therapies.

You will not be surprised to learn,(if you don't already know), that there is confusion about what the word 'Healing' infers. There are many types of healing, which come under the generic term 'Healing'. These are: Spiritual-Healing, Faith healing, Distant or Absent-Healing, Etheric-Healing, Auric-field-healing and Chakra-healing.

There is also the ability of the healer to heal through words. Sometimes it is through the vibration of the voice that healing comes about.

Basically, there are only two camps; Faith-healing is really on its own by demanding that the person receiving the healing, has faith in it and it usually involves particular religious beliefs according to which sect is administering the healing. Faith healing is usually associated with 'charismatic' sects inside or outside mainstream Christian churches. And usually involves ritual of some kind.

Spiritual healing does not ask the receiver to believe that it will work. In the sanctuary where my wife and I worked as healers for many years, a goodly proportion of the patients came only as a last resort, when orthodox medicine had either failed or given them up. They came through recommendation, but I would say that many were very sceptical on their first arrival at the clinic. I would also say that although spiritual-healing works without the belief of the recipient, it does work better if the belief is there.

So, what is spiritual healing? Even this is open to a wide variety of opinion; particularly among the healers themselves. Most people believe that they channel the healing energies through the benevolence of a caring and intelligent 'God force'. Many healers accept the Christian master 'Jesus', whilst others just accept that there is something outside of our scope of understanding, which enables the healing energies to be channelled. My own preference is to call this being, 'The God-Force'. I wouldn't dare to attempt any description of this force because it is beyond my own understanding. I also accept that there are masters, such as Jesus, Buddha etc. who direct their followers in their work upon the Earth plane.

As well as believing in a 'Supreme Being' who allows the use of the healing energies, many also accept that the energies are channelled by 'guides' from the 'Spirit-World'. These guides know how to use the energies and how to 'plug them in' to the healer, also known as the 'Instrument'. Most of these guides, at least in Britain, are indigenous North Americans. Possibly, because we, in this country, have an affinity with these great people. I know that I spent my childhood making bows and arrows and crawling around in the long grass with my sisters and my friends.

As well as these natural healers from North America and. of course, from elsewhere, there are also spirit doctors nurses etc. many of whom are specialists in different fields. The lady, who ran the sanctuary where my wife and I were trained, had a psychiatrist guide and a guide who specialised in healing animals. (He had been a vet whilst on the Earth plane).

There are a few healers who do not believe in anything but their own natural ability to channel the healing energies. Indeed, there are people who have the psychic ability to do just that, drawing the energy from the earth and/or the cosmos. There is a danger with some people in that the energy, which they use comes from their own bodies and auras and they fall prey to sickness themselves. They usually give up healing after a short while. I did know one healer who worked whilst she had a very bad heart condition. This lady unknowingly sucked energy from her patients into herself. At the end of a healing session she was glowing with energy whilst her poor patients were totally drained. Unfortunately, knowing no better, they all thought that the healing was marvellous because they felt so exhausted. It has to be said here, that people can feel very relaxed after healing and, indeed, if their energies have been put right, they can feel tired.

As to the other types of healing mentioned earlier, these all come under the generic term 'Spiritual-Healing' and are mostly self-explanatory. Distant-healing and Absent-Healing are classed as one and the same by some people, being the ability to send healing to people anywhere on the planet, and I know from first hand experience that this type of healing is very effective, and, at times, more so than touch healing. Distant-healing is considered, by some, to be where the patient and healer are in the same room, but the healer is seated a little way away. This is the situation when I do "Attunement" healing.

Most Spiritualist healers are taught that healing power is "The Passive Power". I dispute this because the whole object of healing is to effect a change, for the better, of the physical, emotional and spiritual well being of the recipient. Therefore, if a change is brought about, the power cannot be passive. What should be 'passive', is the healer; the more the healer, "keeps out of the way" of the healing process, the better the quality of the healing. It is like the difference between a conductor and a super-conductor. There is an amount of resistance in the first, and virtually no resistance in the second. The healer must put aside the ego and be passive to the energy flowing through to ensure the best quality of healing.

This is why many healers prefer 'trance-healing' to any other sort of healing. It has to be said, that the same is true of clairvoyant mediumship. The more that the medium surrenders their will to the spirit world, the better their mediumship becomes. Too many mediums allow their own mind to affect the evidence and/ or message from a communicator.

It must be said that the human body is its best healer. All the mechanisms are there for self -healing. There is, of course, the immune system but there is also an esoteric healing mechanism within the body for self- repair. When the body gets to a point where it is so lacking energy that it cannot repair itself, the healer can provide the energy so that the body can repair itself.

When someone receives a shock, whether physically or emotionally, the aura will lose energy from the area at the bottom of the spine, between the hips. This is a safety valve point so that the aura does not suffer damage. Normally, the body seals off the area and will gradually recover. If the shock is great and the problems persist, the seepage of energy continues, to the detriment of the health of the patient; lack of energy in the aura can cause further health problems. Healers, placing their hands over the area can seal in the energies. If energy is leaking from this area, a cool draught can be felt coming from the body. We had a patient at the sanctuary, who had been on anti-depressants for 20 years, after the birth of a child. She travelled all the way from Hampshire for healing. After two sessions of correcting her energies and sealing of the leakage of energy, she was able to stop taking the tablets.

Over the years, I have noticed that many people, while receiving healing, turn their palms upwards. Often, they are just copying what they have seen other people doing but sometimes they have been erroneously taught this. There are chakra points in the palms through which the energy flows. When the healer is giving energy, the energy flows out through the palms. People practising Tai Chi or Chi gung will recognise this. A master of these arts can send a person flying across the room by channelling energy through the palms. Thus, if you are receiving healing, the hands should be clasped together or placed flat on the thighs. Turning the palms upwards allows the healing energies to flow down your arms and out of your palms. Yogis, when practicing the lotus position will have palms upwards but with index fingers and thumbs touching so that the energy is kept within the system.

In respect of the actual healing energies themselves, there are differing thoughts on this. There are many people who say that all healing comes from God and is the same whoever channels it. I do not subscribe to this theory, myself, as it is obvious that some healers achieve much better results than others. However, I do believe that the more spiritually evolved the healer, the higher the energies are which can be channelled through. One has only to consider the miracles wrought by the master Jesus, (or Joshua in the Hebrew), to see that there is a wide disparity in the effectiveness of healers. As I said previously, I do believe that we work under the auspices of the Masters on the 13th plane of existence, (some people would say the 7th plane). However, to achieve the highest standards of healing, takes many life times of existence on the Earth-plane.

The most commonly used healing energy is from the Earth itself. This comes under the general term of 'Mental Energy'. The source of this energy is mainly from the Ley-line system and is basically the magnetic energy of the Earth itself. The Ley-line system encircles the globe and has nodal points in various places, which are known as energy centres. Healers, as well as psychics, can tap into the ley-line energy for their work.

Where such work is carried-out habitually, an energy centre develops. This energy centre is usually in the shape of a cross within a circle. Another source of mental-energy is from the cosmos around us. It is the energy from which everything is made from matter to thought; The Chinese call it chi, the Japanese ki and the Asian Indians, Prana. Many people concentrate on using this energy alone, drawing it down through the top of the head to the feet, often whilst imagining a colour. There is dispute as to what is the colour of the general healing energy. Many claim it to be blue, others, green and some others, white. This comes down to a matter of perception on the part of the individual rather than on any absolute. When I am giving or sending healing, the colours come to me rather than by deliberate effort on my part. As well as the aforementioned basic colours, I see red, orange and, mostly, purple or violet, but, sometimes, I see gold or silver. This can depend upon the energy centre, which is being used at the time, (see the section on chakras).

Akin to the magnetic healing energy, is electric-energy. This energy is useful for stimulating nerve growth after strokes or accidents. It is used very rarely.

Even more rarely used, is 'Physical-energy'. This energy is very powerful and is managed from the spirit side by very advanced guides or doctors. It is the energy, which can effect miraculous cures on seemingly hopeless cases. Healers who can channel this energy can dissolve tumours and perform other miracles of healing. Physical energy is also used, under special conditions, for materialisations and the like, where spirit is able to take solid form and speak so that all present can hear.

Etheric-healing and Auric-field-healing use mental energy. The etheric body is the inner part of the aura and is connected to the etheric counterparts of all of the physical organs. The etheric and auric field bodies are made-up from both Earth and cosmic energy.

It might be thought that healing is such a complicated thing that only highly skilled specialists are able to do it. Nothing of the sort; if one keeps to just 'Touch-healing', it is possible for anyone on the planet to heal. It is best for beginners to touch only the head, (hands either side at the temples), and the shoulders; the healing-energies can flow to the needy areas from these points.

Everybody, then, has the ability to give healing: most people don't for a variety of reasons such as; 'Healing is only possible because healers have a special gift' or, 'I would be a healer if I had the time'. If you feel that healing is really beyond you, then you can send healing-thoughts or prayers to family, friends or people who you hear about on the news. As I said previously, 'Absent-healing' is often as good and sometimes more effective than 'touch-healing'.

If you feel that you would like to give healing to close friends or family, then begin by having a short period of quiet. Then, say a prayer to whatever you believe in for the healing-energies to filter through and, if you like, put on some soft music to bring in a calming vibration. Healing is done, preferably, with the receiver facing southward; to align with the Earth's magnetic field.

When I begin healing, I always say a prayer,(silently), for the individual who is to receive. If you wish to do any more than hands on head or shoulders, then it is imperative that you should seek training from healers with recognised qualifications. Believe me, it is possible for things to go wrong if you do things that you might have seen performed by a healer in a television programme or at a demonstration. When I did my training, the basic-healing course was over two years twice weekly for 36-40 weeks per year. After that, we had another five years and then, I must say, the learning never stops. Working as a healer, full-time or part-time requires a lot of dedication.

The effects of healing can be difficult to define. Although I have witnessed "miracle" cures, over the years; i.e. instantaneous healing, mostly, patients have to attend several sessions. Some patients with chronic health problems attend for prolonged periods. One such case was a man who had had to give up working because of his chronic arthritis. On his first visit he was using a walking stick for support but after the healing, he discarded this aid.

He was a man in his seventies and did hard manual work which he loved. He continued coming for healing until his death several years later but he carried on working to the end and his arthritis never bothered him again.

Healing is very beneficial for those who are destined to depart this life. My wife and I were administering healing to a lady who had terminal cancer. Her father, who had come over from Austria to be with her, was so grateful that his daughter had a peaceful ending to her life; unlike his wife who had suffered from exactly the same problem and had a very troubled ending.

Sometimes the first effect of healing is on a subtle, spiritual level. The person might still suffer pain but they are more uplifted and positive. If they continue to receive healing, then they begin to benefit more on a physical level and pain can diminish or disappear altogether.

Many people who receive healing can have their life improved even if the health problem remains. They will probably have their ups and downs but will be able to cope much better than if they received no healing.

There is always the occasional person who does not benefit. Often this is because they don't give it a chance or their negativity blocks the healing process, but sometimes, it seems, that they are not destined to get better. Some people hang on to their illness as a crutch to support them in life. They will get better but when told that they are so well that they don't need to come so often, they go back to square one and tell you that they need to keep coming.

Many people use music when they give healing; either so-called 'Classical' music or so-called 'New-Age' music. (To a musician involved in 'Serious' or 'High-brow' music, neither title would be deemed correct). The music is used to calm and soothe the patient or to help calm-down the vibrations of the room to allow the use of higher healing energies. Often, particular pieces of music can have beneficial effects upon certain conditions. I use my own especially composed music when healing or meditating, but often, silence is just as valid. Personally, I think that a lot of music used by healers is distracting to both healer and recipient, but then, every individual is different. Music, which does not have wide variations of volume, is best because you are less likely to be startled or drawn out of a meditative state when the music is on a more even keel.

There are, then, many opinions among healers as to what is healing and, what the healing energies, are, and from whence they originate. Only further study and practice can persuade any individual as to what they themselves believe; many find that as time goes by, their own beliefs change in the light of new knowledge and or experience.

Before closing this section, I would like to state that, although I feel that the alleviation of pain and suffering, and the curing of dis-ease, is a very important part of healing, I believe that the more important part of healing is the help which the spirit receives, not only in respect of the calming of the spirit and a helping to cope, but also for the help which recipients of healing are given in making steps forward along their spiritual pathways. Many patients end-up as healers themselves and most gain, at least, some knowledge of spirit and cosmic law.

As a final point, many of the mediums I know, have said that the healing gift is the highest gift. I feel that this is belittling their own contribution to the healing process. I have known many people saved from despair and even suicide through the receiving of a timely message from a medium promising, at least, hope for their future.

In itself, this is a form of healing because it helps the recipient to be more positive and to feel more uplifted thereby bringing about an improvement in their well being.


SELF HEALING

Self-healing is, perhaps, the most difficult sort of healing to practice. Certainly, most people I know would agree with that. Either, one tends to concentrate too hard, or one falls asleep quite quickly. Often, it is more difficult to visualise colour when self-healing, as opposed to giving touch healing to someone else. Again, most colours can be used in self-healing visualisation.

Self-healing can be practised standing, sitting or lying-down. If you lie down, it is best to lie on the back with the knees bent and the feet placed flat on the floor. if you can't place your feet flat, don't worry, just lie completely flat. All forms of healing are best practiced facing South. This is so that your body's magnetic energy- field lines-up with the magnetic energy-field of the Earth. It is essential that you feel comfortable whichever position you choose and that you wear loose, comfortable clothing. Why not try all three positions to see which suits you best? Of course, there are times when one position is more appropriate than another. It is also essential to ask for healing and to link in with the healing energies, from whatever force you believe in: God, The God-force, Mother-Earth, etc. It is also good to ask for protection. There are many who do not believe this to be so, but it is better to be safe than sorry.

Having made yourself comfortable, and said your prayer, you might wish to use a relaxation technique to make yourself more receptive to the energies.

The most common of these techniques is to imagine the various parts of your body going to sleep, starting with the toes and working upwards. You might do each toe individually if you wish. You could imagine little men, who work the various parts of the body, tucking themselves up in bed and nodding-off. Don't overdo it or you could find yourself asleep very quickly.

When you feel that you are sufficiently relaxed, you can ask for the energies to be applied. Some people imagine the energy coming up through the feet; others prefer to draw it from above the head down into the body. For beginners, it makes sense to draw through the feet as (see previous chapter), this is the most natural way. Whichever way you draw the energy, you might feel a sensation of coolness or tingling or just have an awareness that it is happening but whichever it is, proceed slowly for the best results. Sometimes it is easier to imagine the energy as a liquid being drawn up from a lake or similar or even that your feet are immersed in healing waters in a bowl, with your legs acting like straws or the capillaries in plants. As you draw-in the energy, imagine that it is further relaxing each part in turn. Imagine your body feeling cleansed and feeling good. You might also feel the negativity being washed out of the body into the ground to be transmuted into (as I do), golden energy.

Let the energy rise slowly, embracing all the internal organs, the bones the arteries, veins and capillaries etc. cleaning and repairing as it goes. You might also work on a microcosmic scale, visualising all the cells, atoms and molecules being cleaned and becoming bright and healthy. Having directed the healing throughout the entire body, try to perceive the body as from across the room, glowing with health, being lighter and cleaner, feeling good and feeling healthy. Some people like to draw in the cosmic energy as well as the earth energy; this can be done after or even at the same time.

To draw in the cosmic energies, begin exactly as before, but instead of drawing the energies up through the feet, imagine a golden or white cloud about two feet above your head. You can then imagine either rain falling from the clouds and filling-up your body with healing energy, or imagine the cloud itself descending slowly to envelop the body and its mists penetrating the body to heal and cleanse as per above. In the oriental system of chi-gung, it is thought that the cosmic energies entering through the top of the head is a more gentle way of healing. This is because Earth energies are, in fact, a concentrated form of cosmic energy.

White is a good energy to visualise because it contains all the colours of the spectrum and appropriate colours will be drawn naturally to where they are needed.

# CHAPTER NINE

## THE SUBTLE ENERGIES OF THE PHYSICAL BODY

Perhaps the most well known subtle energy field is the 'auric-field'. The aura is invisible to the majority of people because of the very high frequencies at which it vibrates. The aura starts about six inches or so away from the body. Closer to, and within, the body are the' etheric' bodies and the 'chakras'.

The aura is made-up of many layers and contains all the data, which we, as spiritual and material beings, require. A good auric-field reader can tell you all about yourself from pre-birth to the far future. All is recorded there: health, character, emotional nature and all of those things, which give rise to opportunities of spiritual growth. A good, healthy aura can range over several feet, and the aura of an 'adept 'or of a 'master', can range infinitely further. The aura can be very colourful in a healthy, spiritual person.

Various colours in the auric field denote different things. Green at the front or back of the head can denote that the person is a healer; green to the sides of the head would indicate that the person was receiving healing. Many people consider that blue is the healing colour, but that, of course, is a matter of how each person perceives the vibrations. It is true to say, however, that all colours can be used in healing, depending upon the nature of the healing required, and the ability of the healer to channel the necessary healing vibration.

The aura is derived from two types of energy; "Earth" energy and "Cosmic" energy.

The Earth energy is drawn-up through our feet at the point known to Orientals as the "Bubbling spring". In Qi-Gung, it is generally known as the "Foot gate". This energy circulates through the chakra system providing energy for the various body systems as it goes.

The cosmic energy is white light, which emanates from the 'Golden Bowl' at the top of the aura; this is our connection to the "Higher-Self" or spiritual aspect of our being. The white light separates (as through a prism), into the colours of the rainbow; red and orange for the two inner layers, and then, yellow, green, blue, indigo and violet.

As the energy enters the Crown Chakra from above, it flows into the left and right channels through which the cosmic energy flows to all parts of the body, the chakras and the aura. As well as the left and right channels, there is also the Central Channel.

Close to the body is the etheric layer, which inter penetrates the physical body and connects to the physical organs of the body in order to feed them with nourishment from the mental energy source. Each organ of the body, is surrounded by its own etheric body. This is why people can still feel the sensation of having a limb for quite a while after it has been amputated. The etheric body can normally seen as a smoky grey mist.

The third set of subtle energy bodies is the 'chakra system'. Chakra is the Sanskrit word for wheel. . Respectively: root, sacral solar plexus, heart, throat, brow and crown. (Recently, some authors have suggested that more chakras have opened-up in modern man. From my own experience, I am inclined to agree. The chakra system is responsible for distributing the energies to the various body systems: e.g. the root is the energy centre for sexual functions, the sacral chakra is responsible for the water elements in the body and sexual functions while the solar-plexus, (the lower mind), is responsible for the eyes. The chakras have many other, more subtle, functions.

The root is concerned with the sense of smell, the sacral, with taste, the solar plexus with sight and the throat with sound as well as being the 'organ' for the receiving of clairaudiance. The heart chakra is the seat of the emotional body. (Actually, all chakras have a link to the emotions; principally the Sacral, Solar-plexus and Heart). The closer to the root, the more primitive the emotion. Thus, love can be expressed through the heart and throat chakra, nervousness in the solar plexus and fear through the sacral and root chakras. The brow chakra is of the higher-mind and is also responsible for the receiving of clairvoyance. The crown chakra is our link with the Higher self. These are just a few of the main functions of the chakra system; Again, the main chakra points vibrate to the colours of the rainbow. I ought to point out that there is also a chakra at the perineum which points downwards to receive the earth energy coming in from beneath the feet.

More detail is given in a later chapter.

Every being on Earth can, thus, be seen as a system of colour. Like fingerprints, each aura is as individual as is each person. It is said that everybody has a different note and that when they are ready to begin on their spiritual pathway, this note sounds in the spheres and help will be sent to them through spirit-guides. As you may imagine, this means that there are an incalculable number of vibrations in existence.

Many people have postulated that the seven-note scale, i.e. the musical 'Major' scale, can be equated with the seven main chakras. This is absurd, as we shall see.

## COLOUR

Colour is something of which we are constantly aware. When we get-up in the morning, we look in our wardrobes, shirt drawers etc. to find something to wear which might match our mood of the day or bring some upliftment. There might be several factors in our choice but probably the most dominant one is colour. We are very sensitive to colour: I remember, many years ago when undergoing a very stressful time, I used to take myself off to the nearby park to absorb the wonderfully healing vibration of the green grass and the foliage of the trees and bushes. I also got upliftment from seeing the various colours of the roses which almost called-out to me as I passed, "Cheer up, the world is beautiful". Somehow, those trips to the park kept me going and no one, not even my wife, realised how close I was to the edge.

Such a powerful phenomenon, so readily available, cannot be ignored as a therapy, but we must ask, 'What is colour, and how is it able to affect our moods, brighten our lives and give us healing'?

Colour is part of the electromagnetic spectrum, which radiates from the Sun. This spectrum includes: radio waves, microwaves, infra-red waves, visible light waves and X-rays. We are able to see only the visible light waves, but we do not see them directly. It is only when light is reflected from an object that we see colour. When light strikes against an object, most of it is absorbed by the object. What the object does not absorb is reflected out and picked-up by receptors in the eyes so that we see the object as being red, green, blue etc.

The vibratory speed of light is phenomenally fast; the oscillation between peaks can be 5000,000,000,000,000. i.e. the wave moves backwards and forwards that many times between peaks. (Some might say, up and down).

Colour healing was mentioned in an earlier chapter but I feel it is right to iterate that what we see as colour is a perception in the brain. Not everybody sees the same colour when they look at an object. This is the reason for 'colour blindness'.

Often healers say that they channel certain colours for certain conditions. I feel that it is appropriate to just set the intention to heal and ask for the healing energies to flow. Higher minds than ours know what is appropriate. As healers, we may perceive colours as the energies flow but remember, energy is a vibration not a colour. As an example, the Sun pours out lots of different vibrations, some perceived as colour and some perceived as heat and a lot more not perceived by us at all. It all hinges on our receptors.

Colour in the room, however, can enhance, or otherwise, the healing session. Pastel shades are more soothing than vibrant colours. Sometimes the patients can be advised to wear more colourful clothes. People who are depressed often wear black or other dull colours. (Black in conjunction with some other colours is fine and often striking to the eye.)

# CHAPTER TEN

## ATTACHMENTS

Over the years, I have often been asked to remove attachments from people. Attachments are spirits, which attach themselves to a person and cause them to think or do "bad" things. Mediums should NEVER tell anyone that they have an attachment. I have known this happen; it is grossly irresponsible and could leave the person with a problem for life.

The Spiritualist's point of view, which I share, is that it doesn't happen in the way that people think it does. Most people talk about "Possession" where some malignant spirit inhabits the body of the possessed person. Such things, most often, are in the mind of the person who think they are possessed or have an attachment. Often it is just to do with their ego, similar to having their own ghost.

What I would say is, that people draw beings of a similar nature to themselves. If one is helpful and kind, then that is the sort of spirit, which would be drawn to the person.

People who are malicious, unkind, etc, would, possibly, but only possibly, draw a malicious spirit to themselves. These spirits can influence people by sending out thoughts to them, dragging them down even further.

In all cases of this sort, I always send absent healing to the person.

They will always hang on to their affliction and will try to persuade the healer that they, indeed, do have an attachment. They usually wear it like a badge of distinction.

There is nothing in the Spirit World that can persuade anybody to do anything that they don't want to do. Often, it is just a cry for help or attention.

I was asked to visit a house in which the occupants were convinced that there were malignant spirits. After doing the energies of the house, I said that the couple should only play gentle music and should refrain from watching horror films and the like. "There you are", said the lady, "I told you not to watch those horror movies after you came back from the pub." I was very annoyed that I'd been summoned at short notice, by these people, and had missed a friend's anniversary celebration in so doing.

Never be taken in by someone who tells you that they have an attachment. If they are not just seeking attention of some kind, they ought to see a psychiatrist.

# CHAPTER ELEVEN

## MUSIC AND HEALING

The most common explanation of music is, that it is 'organised sound', but, one might ask, "What is sound"? Whilst we were studying the nature of music, during a lecture at college, our head of department posed the question,

"If there was an organ playing with all the stops out in a church, and there was no one present in the building, what would be the sound"? There were many and varied replies to this, none of which I can remember. I do, however, remember the answer. There would be no sound; this astonished us all but it is something, which I took to heart.

I once gave a talk on "Music and Healing", beginning with the proposition that there is no such thing as sound. This astonished my listeners and they were eager to hear the explanation.

Sound begins as a motion: a dustbin lid falling off, a wave lapping against the side of a boat and other such natural phenomena. The striking of one object against another causes ripples in the air, (sound-waves), just as a stone thrown into a pond causes ripples. The ripples in the air are known as 'sound-waves'. There is no sound, however, until the waves have passed through the outer ear and into the inner ear to cause another vibration in the hearing apparatus, i.e. the ear-drum etc. which, in turn, causes an electrical current to be sent to the brain. Until this message reaches the brain, there is, therefore, no sound. This becomes obvious when we hear of people who are 'stone-deaf'. The vibration reaches their ears just as it does to those of hearing people, but, because their hearing apparatus is faulty, no sound is heard. It is in the brain, therefore, that sound is manifested.

(To give a little more information: it is the collision of atoms and molecules, which make the ripples in various media.)

In music, a variety of methods are used to cause sound: Stringed instruments, can be bowed or plucked, percussion instruments are struck in a number of different ways, wind instruments apart from the flute family and the brass section have a reed to initiate the sound. Brass instruments utilise the vibrating lips of the player to cause the sound.

Music is not only 'organised sound' but, there is a qualitative difference between what is called sound, and what is called noise. Within a sound, whether it be noise or otherwise), many frequencies occur. When a dustbin lid falls to the ground or when a door is slammed, noise is caused. The vibrations of noise are haphazard, with frequencies building up or dying away at differing intervals of time. The 'envelope' (as it is known), of an instrumental sound is much more controlled. Any sound, however made, is a combination of many sounds, with one dominant sound, which is the main one we hear. In music, this sound, or note, is called the 'fundamental'. This fact is very important, as we shall see later.

What is true of sound is also true of other types of vibration, or energies, which our 'sense-receptors' convert into signals for our brains to interpret. Colour, for example, is the result of objects reflecting one of the colours from the spectrum of white light. The other colours are absorbed by the object in question. Thus, light rays from the sun (or from an artificial source), strike an object, which absorbs some of the light vibrations and reflects others. The object itself, therefore, is not coloured', what we see as colour is the reflected light waves. We can only perceive this colour if we have the correct receiving apparatus and de-coder. Dogs, for example, are said to be able to see only in grey: they can, however, hear much higher pitched sounds than we, and their sense of smell, in comparison to ours, is phenomenal. Humans can only hear sounds vibrating between 16 to 20,000 cycles per second. Once again, what we hear is dependent upon the quality of our receiving apparatus.

If I were to be cruel, I could quote chunks from a musical dictionary to prove my point, but I will try to paraphrase part of the section on acoustics from the ' Harvard Dictionary of Music'. "The generation of sound is bound-up with the vibration of an elastic body." It goes on to talk about 'kinetic energy' etc. So, sound starts as a form of energy through the vibration of an object and in turn, sound waves are formed in the air and travel to our receptors, which translate the vibrations into electrical signals to send to the brain.

To summarise, then, sound and other sense-phenomena are the products of our own organs of perception, converted into sense sensations in the brain. As can be seen, these phenomena exist in nature as different types of energies or vibrations.

# MUSIC AND COLOUR

When people (non musicians) ascribe colours to music they are usually referring to a correspondence of colour to pitch, and I have often heard people suggesting that there is a correspondence between the chakras and the scale of 'C', but this is nonsense, as we shall see. Pitch is very hard to define without reference to terms which are not really relevant to sound, but to something more concrete. Thus, pitch is thought of as being 'High' or 'Low'. A flute is a high pitched instrument and a tuba is a low pitched instrument. Pitch is determined by how many times a second a sound wave vibrates.

If you were to take a tuning fork pitched in 'A', and strike the fork against your knee or some where which wouldn't damage you or the fork, it would vibrate at 440 cycles per second, i.e. 440 times per second. This is the note upon which orchestras are tuned and, consequently, is said to be in 'Concert Pitch'. This pitch is internationally accepted by convention. (If you held the fork close to, but not touching, your ear, you would feel the vibrations of the air striking your ear).

However, the pitch of any given note is not absolute or inviolate. The modern day 'concert pitch' of 'A = 440', has been accepted internationally only since 1960. Prior to this, different regions had different pitch standards. Europe, for example, used the pitch 'A' = 435 cps. Victorian instruments were pitched at 'A' = 480cps.

At the time of the great J.S.Bach, three different pitches were in use at the same time. 'Church' pitch, 'Concert-hall' pitch and 'Town band' pitch. The noise when the town band passed a performance at a church or concert hall must have been horrendous.

If the aforementioned were not enough, there are other factors to take into consideration. The principal factor being that modern music is based on an artificial system of equal semitones; aptly named, "Equal Temperament". This was introduced at the time of J S. Bach, and was promoted by him in his, well-known work: The Well Tempered Klavier (piano). Before this time, there were different systems in use, based on calculations by Pythagoras who experimented with vibrating strings.

Explanations of the various systems are too complex to worry us in a book such as this; suffice to say, the present system is not based upon that which exists in nature,('Just Temperament) but is artificially designed in order to promote facility in changing from one key to another. Previously, it was only possible to modulate to 'closely related' keys, but now modulation to any key is possible, (however tortuous the route). In Equal Temperament, no interval other than the octave is acoustically correct.

Another point to consider when designating colours to musical notes or musical notes to chakra vibrations, is the fact that many cultures use microtones in their musical systems; Middle-Eastern music, Indian music, etc. There are thirteen semitones in an Equal temperament major scale. Each semitone can be divided into 100cents. This means that for each semitone, there are 100 possible divisions. There are, therefore, many more possible notes in a scale. There are only five notes in the pentatonic scales, which were in use in China around 2000BC, and can be considered as the prototype for all scales. (The pentatonic scale can be heard by playing just the black notes on a piano).

If you consider the rainbow, and then a piano keyboard, you will see that it does not make sense to designate all the colours of the rainbow to just one octave in the middle of the piano. The colours of the rainbow are spread in bands; which would suggest that the same ought to be true if you equate sound waves with light waves. It would make more sense to assign a band of one colour to one octave of music rather than to one note.

Many composers pride themselves on the use of colour in their compositions. This 'colouring' is achieved through orchestration; i.e. the mixing or blending of different 'tone-colours', in respect of the instruments used. The composer sees him or her self as an artist, with a blank sheet of paper and a palette, mixing e.g. flutes with horns or oboes with flutes etc. This is orchestral colouring.

Thus, we can see that different instruments are thought to have different tone colours. A recorder, for example, is the least 'colourful' of instruments and has the simplest waveform (almost like a sine-wave). Compare this with the rich fruity tones of the lower register of the clarinet and you can see that to try to equate the two instruments in respect of colour is really nonsensical. In the talk which I gave, I was able to illustrate this by actually playing the same sequence of notes on different instruments and people were able to grasp what I was saying much more readily than without the hearing experience.

Different instruments have different characters: trumpets can be bright and triumphant, oboes plaintive and melancholy, bassoons are often used in comical passages. Different combinations of instruments, also, can produce a wide variety of moods.

If you can, try to hear as many different instruments as you can; you will really appreciate the differing tone-colours. Benjamin Britten's, "Young Person's Guide to the Orchestra" is a good piece of music to listen to in order to appreciate the different 'colours' of the orchestra.

The reason, acoustically, for the range of colour among the families of instruments is due to what are called, 'overtones' or 'partials (and sometimes, "harmonics"). When a note is sounded, one hears the 'fundamental' of the note. For example, if the note 'C' is sounded, then you hear the note 'C'. What the ear does not discriminate, are the notes contained within that note. Thus, the note consists of, not only the frequency of the fundamental, but also many other frequencies which the ear does not pick up as notes but which enrich the fundamental note, giving it its particular tone. The factors, which give rise to the differentiation in tone are, size, shape, material of construction and method of sound production. For example, when a trumpet is sounded, the sound is produced by the vibration of the player's lips, whereas, when a clarinet or oboe is played, the sound is initiated by the vibration of the reed. These factors all affect which overtones are dominant in the sound produced.

If you have a piano, you can try the following experiment: hold down the note 'C' above 'middle C' and then strike 'middle C' sharply letting go immediately. You should hear the higher note sounding sympathetically. Then try it again with the notes 'G', 'E' and the 'C' above. You should be able to hear the higher notes in each case. The higher notes are, of course, the 'overtones' or 'partials'.

One must also consider, when thinking of colour in music, of the juxtaposition of one note against another either played singly or together. Without going into technical details such as Major, Minor, Augmented intervals etc., it can be appreciated that some notes following each other, (or sounding together), sound 'sweet'. Whilst, others sound strange or even unpleasant. (In ancient times, the interval of an augmented fourth was called "The Devil in Music"). Before our system of scales came into being, there was a system called the 'Modal Scale System'. This was a system in which each of the scales was different to every other scale. (Our folksongs were based on the modal system). In ancient times, each modal scale was thought to have its own, particular magical properties and the scales were used in ceremonies for this purpose.

Again, if you have a piano, play eight notes in a row using only the white notes. If you start on the note 'C', you will, of course, be playing a scale of 'C Major'. If you play eight notes from 'D' to the 'D' above, you will be playing the 'Dorian' mode. 'E' is the 'Phrygian' mode, 'F' is the 'Lydian' mode etc.

What you will notice above all, is how strange they sound and how different they are from each other, particularly if you are able to play chords in the mode

The reason that I have given this detail, is to illustrate that, in the general run of things, notes cannot be taken in isolation. Everything that vibrates affects and is affected by other vibrations giving rise to a huge variety of relationships, which could be termed 'tone-colour'.

Another type of colouring in music is called chromaticism, (from the Greek 'chromos' which means, colour). This is the use of notes, which do not naturally occur in the scale or key being used. For example, the scale of 'C major', consists of all 'naturals', i.e. there are no sharps or flats in the scale. If a sharp or flat is introduced into the music, this would be called a 'chromatic' note and it would bring about a change of 'colour' into the piece of music.

I think that the foregoing is as much as is necessary to convince anyone that, it would be really impossible to designate any specific musical note a specific colour from the rainbow spectrum. I will now very briefly explain why a seven note musical scale,(as we know it) would not make much sense as a correlation with the chakra system. In the scale of "C Major" (starting from the C above Middle C), each note in Equal Temperament vibrates (in cycles per second), as follows :

| C | d | e | f | g | a | d | C |
|-----|-----|-----|-----|-----|-----|-----|------|
| 520 | 584 | 655 | 694 | 779 | 874 | 982 | 1040 |

You can see that a note at the octave vibrates at twice the speed of the note an octave below.

From different sources, one of which is Peter Rendell's book, "Introduction to the Chakras, (Another source was an old friend of mine, Florence Jemi, who obtained the information whilst in trance and gave a very interesting lecture on the subject.) I quote here the vibratory rates of the chakras in ascending order from the root to the crown:

4   6   10   12   16   96   960

If you compare this set of vibrations with the major scale you will see that they by no means marry-up. Taking the first set of figures as a standard musical scale (which it is), the step from the first chakra to the second chakra (in respect of its vibratory rate) is the same, approximately, as the distance between the first 'C' of the scale and the note 'g' which is the fifth note of the musical scale. by the third number in the chakra scale the octave has already been passed. At the fifth chakra we would have a musical note two octaves above the first note of the scale; we then have a leap from the fifth chakra to the sixth, which brings us nearly five octaves above the first chakra. As we get to the tremendous leap to the last chakra,(nearly 8 octaves above the first ), I will rest my case.

When music is played, or sounds are made, an energy is put into motion through the vibration of atoms existing in the sound production unit of the instrument. This vibration moves through the air and enters our ears to strike against the ear-drum. Sound, therefore, has no intrinsic quality of its own but is simply waves of energy moving through the air. Light,(and therefore, colour), on the other hand, does have its own intrinsic qualities. It is matter given-off from a heat source such as the Sun and other stars. There is also a fundamental difference between sound and light in that the former moves only in wave form, (as far as scientists can tell at the moment), whereas light exists as both particle and wave.

If all of the foregoing leads you to believe that I think that colour and sound cannot be equated in some way, then you would be wrong. I think that I am trying to point - out that simplistic notions of convergences of sound and colour do not hold water.

Light, vibrates at a very much higher frequency than sound and its waves are infinitesimally smaller, however, it is possible through the receptors that we have in our psychic bodies for there be an equation between the two.

Note: Light vibrates at between 5-7,000,000,000,000,000,000 oscillations per second and has wave lengths around 1/20,000th. of a centimetre, whereas sound discerned by the human ear is between 16 cycles per sec and 20.000 cps.

# MUSIC

Music exists as a special type of energy. It is heard through the hearing apparatus of the human ear on the material plane, but it is experienced quite differently according to the senses on the different planes of existence above the material plane.

As material and spiritual beings, we can experience music on various levels via the different 'bodies' we possess. The most obvious of these, being the "emotional" body. When we experience music through the emotional body, our moods can change quite dramatically.

Listening to a symphony, for example, we can experience quite a wide range of emotion in a comparatively short space of time.

Each individual will tune-in more harmoniously with particular types of music; other music might jar, irritate or cause other unpleasant affects. So, while some people might feel uplifted by a Beatles number or by a particular type of popular music, others will feel more at ease with Beethoven or Bartok.

It would be difficult to comprehend how music affects the non-material bodies just as it would be difficult for a non-psychic to comprehend the gifts of mediumship, which are, in fact, merely other senses which all human beings have but which are not yet 'open ' in the majority of the population. Nonetheless, music is a very potent force in the material world. American Indian music is rarely performed for just listening to but rather for creating energy for specific purposes. (A visitor to one of the tribes could not get them to sing an hunting song because they weren't hunting at the time). There are songs for treating the sick, songs for success in battle, religious songs, ceremonial songs etc.

In the western world, music is used to influence us to buy things or to spend more than we intended through the playing of catchy tunes, which make us feel happy. It is also used to good effect in films or other dramatisations to enhance the mood of any particular moment.

There is also good evidence to suggest that music can affect our physiology for better or for worse and we know that music is used in different therapies for healing purposes.

Music has different components, which act in various ways upon the psyche.

These elements are as follows: pitch, duration, silence and rhythm.

Rhythm acts on a more basic material level such as in march-band music, Jazz and heavy-beat rock music which persuades people to get their limbs and bodies moving in time to the music, (acting upon the root-chakra),but it can also, if lyrical or melodic affect the heart-chakra,( pulling at the heart-strings). I remember, as a teenager, very much into traditional jazz, being upset when a workmate told me that, "Jazz is just syncopated discords". I checked the definition in my dictionary and was horrified to find that the dictionary agreed with my friend. It wasn't until I studied music many years later, that I discovered that all good music contains syncopation and discords. The great, J.S.Bach was an exponent of such music particularly through the use of those marvellous suspensions bringing such poignance to his music (a suspension is the carrying forward of one note of a chord to the next chord by holding on to it through the use of a 'tie' thereby creating a displacement of the accent, i.e. syncopation, and also discordance in the 2nd chord with the inclusion of a note foreign to that chord).

The duration of a note or chord is important because if it is too long or too short this can cause an imbalance and we can feel annoyed or deprived. On its own, a long note soon gets boring to the human ear and can cause great irritation. Sometimes, of course, a sound, which is pleasing to the ear, is stopped before we have gained full pleasure from it and we feel deprived.

Pitch is, perhaps, the most potent element on the physical side because each pitch(or frequency) has a vibrational energy which is unique, and there are literally millions of them on the material plane. Some act on a sub-atomic level, some on a molecular level and many other levels up to the very long waves, which act on a macrocosmic level. The "Great Breath" is an immensely long wave cycle of 25,000 years. Some very long waves can make the whole body pulse and make you lose balance or feel sick. On the other hand, some, relatively, long waves can soothe and calm, can ease the mind and help you to sleep. A slow wave lap on a shore can induce feelings of tranquillity into your being.

Silence is an important element in music; it is a breathing space for change.

Many of us crave silence for just a little while each day in order to refresh ourselves.

However, the silence, which occurs in many of the great works, is a silence of great power; one can almost hear it, almost feel it pulsing with energy. This energy exists all the time, but can only be appreciated or sensed when no sound waves reach the ear. The great masters (such as gurus or yogi.) are able to meditate in any conditions but some of us mere mortals prefer to meditate in conditions of silence.

What we have most to silence, of course, is not just outside noise but also 'inside noise', i.e. the frenzied activities of our own material minds. Those who teach meditation etc. always say, "Go into the silence".

There are many vibrations, which occur in music, which are not picked-up as individual frequencies by the ear; these are the overtones or partials, which were mentioned in an earlier chapter. As has been said, it is the relative strength, or amplitude, of these frequencies which give instruments their particular 'colour. '(A note sounded on a clarinet will be very different to that of a trumpet or oboe etc. at the same pitch). None of the overtones, with the exceptions of the octaves (2,4,8) are tones of equal temperament but are tones of 'Just Intonation'. A scale of 'Just Intonation' would sound very strange to our modern ears, (see earlier chapter), and, in fact was hardly used being replaced by the system known as the 'Mean-tone' system which would sound equally strange to us. There are in excess of 20 overtones in instrumental sounds,(a recorder, for example, has far fewer and its wave form is very close to that of a sine-wave, which is the simplest wave form). The series of overtones from the fundamental note of 'C' is as follows: 'C' (fundamental), C (octave above), G C E G B flat C D E F sharp G A B flat B natural C (3 octaves above). As you can see, the notes get closer together as the series progresses. This series of overtones, was exploited by Baroque trumpeters using valve less trumpets to play melodies in very high registers. A truly impressive feat as well as sound.

Music is the highly complex organisation of all the above elements. The particular arrangement of these elements will cause specific sounds or energy flows. The energy pattern of a melody can be changed by adding harmony to it or a melody which has already been harmonised can have its energy pattern changed by alterations to the harmony, either through the use of different chordal arrangement or through rhythmic patterns.

# THE MAGIC OF MUSIC

If the 'Magic of Music' means anything, it reflects the ability of music to affect us all in various ways. It can make us feel happy, sad, exhilarated, or calm, contented or relaxed. Many 'alternative' practitioners use music while giving treatments. My own relaxation and healing tapes have been used in this way as well as in hospices to help calm-down the terminally-ill. Many doctors and nurses who have been to the healing clinic where I worked for many years, (The Sanctuary of Progress, run by Linda and Keith Codling), were impressed by the calming effects of the music; some took them away to use for themselves and for their patients. One of the units at an hospital in Brighton used one of the tapes for calming-down the babies in their care.

Advertisers know the power which music has. We are bombarded by advertising jingles, not so much for the words, but more for the catchy tune. In some places it is almost impossible to go into a shop without our ears being assailed by some sort of music or another in order to put shoppers in the mood to part with their hard-earned money.

Music is a very strong focal point in many religions. The psalms and hymns of the Jewish faith, which passed on to the Christian religion, formed a very large part of the early Christian church service and Western music has its very basis in this genre. The psalms and early hymns were written in modes (7 basic types of scale), each one of which was considered to have a different magical property. The modes were thought to invoke magic, and each had a name: Aeolian, Dorian, Lydian, etc. If you play an octave of white notes on the piano, you will be playing a mode. Aeolian is from A to A, Dorian is from D to D. It is the placement of the semi-tones within the scale, which give it its distinct character.

In religions of the Far East, sound is very important. You will all be familiar with the mantras associated with the practice of 'Yoga'. The highest sound vibration is in the word, 'OM' (AUM), representative of the Absolute; Brahman. It is the totality of all sounds and in the Hindu faith it is believed that the whole universe is the result of 'sound'. AUM is also a 'Trinity' (a very sacred concept in several religions). When intoning 'AUM', one begins the sound in the back of the throat, moves it to the front of the mouth and then directs the sound upwards to the top of the head through closing the lips and humming the 'M' part of the sound.

Music, then, is a very powerful force which can affect us emotionally, but can it be used as an healing energy? It can be cathartic as well being able to cause the emotions listed in paragraph one, but I feel that the effects of music can operate on much more subtle levels for healing. I hope to demonstrate this in later chapters of the book, but before this is possible, it is necessary to examine the nature of music so that what is posited has a sound basis scientifically.

Every human being (or animal or mineral etc.) has a unique vibration.

As explained previously, there are millions, at least, of different vibrations existing on the Earth-plane, and not just the vibrations making-up our western musical scales. Every person has their own individual 'note' which is made-up of all the vibrations of which they consist. All of the organs, for example, resonate to their own 'note' as do cells, molecules, atoms etc. as well as the subtle bodies of the individual. It is said that when an individual is ready to take-up spiritual work, then their note is sounded in the spiritual realms and is heard by spirit guides who then travel to the Earth-plane to assist in their development.

An obvious question to ask is, "How can music effect an healing? "The answer is concerned with the nature of matter. We all fondly imagine that everything on the material plane is solid. Scientists will say positively that this is not so.

Everything is made-up of molecules, atoms etc. and if you examine matter under an appropriate microscope it can be seen that there is usually more 'space in an atom than there is matter. The word 'atom' comes from the Greek, 'atomos', which means "unbreakable". However, scientists have discovered, during the 20th. Century, that an atom consists of a nucleus (of protons and neutrons), which is at the centre of an orbiting electron or electrons. The atomic sphere is 10,000 times larger than the nucleus contained within it. If you look, therefore at a diagram of an atom, you will see that there is more space than matter. An atom to a modern scientist, is not the final indivisible particle, but a building block which itself is made-up of smaller particles. Scientists have found that specific atoms vibrate within a narrow spectrum of colour. As the human body is composed of atoms of many different kinds, we must radiate colours like the rainbow from different sections of the body. People, who can see these colours, can tell how healthy a person is by the brightness or lack of it, in the body colours.

All matter consists of countless atoms bound together in various forms to make larger and larger units, some, more dense than others but all having a certain amount of space in their make-up. It is because we have this 'space' in our make-up that music can have healing effects on the material body.

When a musical note or sequence of notes is played, very high frequencies are produced through the partials, (for frequency, read, energy).It is these high frequencies which have a causal effect on the atomic and sub-atomic levels of our bodies and subtle-bodies. (And it is these high frequencies which produce the colours which psychics can perceive). This energy moves through space in the form of sound waves to strike against our bodies. Now, the human body, as previously explained, is more 'space' than 'matter', so it is possible for the very high frequencies to penetrate the body and to have an effect upon individual atoms. Atoms have been seen to vibrate to narrow spectrums of colour so it is logical to assume that if an atom is off-colour', then it is possible through sympathetic resonance, to re-establish its original colour and thus effect an healing. If this seems to be in the realms of fantasy, it is known that when light strikes against certain metals, a release of electrons can occur. This is caused by the particles within the light waves colliding very strongly against the electrons and knocking them out of orbit and right outside of the atom, which they had inhabited. If it can happen with light particles hitting against metal, why can it not also apply to high frequencies of sound striking against human bodies. This can, of course, also happen to matter contained within the auric-field and etheric bodies.(and is likely to happen more frequently). As has been said, our auras store data concerning all that has happened to us from birth; all of our physical problems and our emotional problems. Sometimes, we refuse to let go of problems and we then, draw them from the aura into the etheric body or the physical body. This is, of course, most true of emotional problems. How often do we hear that people are told to let go of the past. In the healing sanctuary where my wife and I worked for many years, they developed a technique of auric-field healing which helped to push past problems further out from the body and into the outer layer of the aura, which holds data much more strongly and, therefore, is less likely to be drawn to the inner layers of the aura or to the body where it could cause problems.

Sometimes, it was possible to remove things from the aura entirely via the discarder layer, which removes unwanted energies. The data was still stored but the negative energy, which it had caused, was removed.

We also cleared-out negative energies from the chakras and cleared blockages in the chakras with similar techniques. This type of energy-blockage removal is, I believe, at the heart of the Japanese healing art of Seiki, which my wife and I had been studying alongside our Chi-Gung practice.

Even when the data is stored in the aura in a layer which is not readily accessible, sometimes there is a residue of the negative energy, which it caused, stuck in a layer from which it can more readily be drawn to cause ongoing problems. These energies can be felt by the physical hand in various ways: e.g. like a wispy material or a little electric current. Music can help to remove these energies from the aura in the manner as previously described, and by creating a more positive emotional state in a person, music can help the person to destroy the unwanted vibration themselves.

Illnesses often begin in the aura. Viruses and the like, for example, can lodge in the aura before they attack the physical body. If they can be removed before they can enter the body, the danger of infection is removed. Sometimes, the auric field energies are affected by a sudden shock to the body, either physical or emotional. The negativity thus caused can adversely affect the physical body causing illness if it is not put right immediately. Thus, it can be seen, the auric field energies can have an effect on the physical body as well as vice versa.

The energies generated by musical sounds, (or vice-versa), will act on the whole-being: physically, emotionally and spiritually through the chakra-system, the auric-field bodies and even upon the cells, atoms and sub-atoms of the body. A beneficial effect will be brought about through 'sympathetic resonance; i.e. a particular wave- form will correspond to a wave form emanating from the human body. For example, if an organ of the body is resonating at a wave-length corresponding to the note 'C', then by playing the note 'C', the organ will be helped to retain its health or to re-establish health if it is diseased.

However, organs and other structures are more complicated than that and might require particular harmonies and rhythms to resonate sympathetically or, they might require certain sequences of notes (e.g. Doh-Me-Soh) repeated frequently during a piece of music.

The following was given to me through inspiration from one of my spirit guides:

Music is food for the soul, enabling the body and spirit to link more closely in vibration. The red vibration gives a warm glow to the body and strength to the spirit.

Blue is the gold on a material level, bringing peace and tranquillity to body and spirit.

Green is the colour of growth, of life-energy and of calming for the spirit and healing for the body. Silver brings purity to body and spirit. The tinkling of a bell brings the colour silver as does the sound of a very high flute.

A full organ sound is red, masculine and authoritative. It bestows power upon the player and the listener. Many colours can be created on the organ; mellow sounds bring yellow and green. Singing, usually, is dominated by pastel shades.

Listening to music will affect the vibrational rate of the body as well as the energies around the body. Music with deep bass rhythms can affect the bio-rhythms of the body and might cause glandular secretions and chemical reactions; either beneficially or adversely. The higher the pitch, the higher the sense affected. This links in with the chakra system and subtle-energy bodies.

Different people might need different music to cure the same complaint. This is because their own vibrational rate is individual to them and their body organs might have different vibrational rates to those of other people, not to mention that their subtle body energies will be different.(End of inspirational passage).

I know that you know how important music is in our modern world. I hope that I have been able to demonstrate how potent music can be in respect of its healing nature and properties. I fully believe that music will take its proper place in healing in the not too distant future but I must emphasize that it should be used as an adjunct to conventional and alternative therapies. Used properly, music can help to aid recovery and shorten illness and in addition, it is very enjoyable to listen to.

# CHAPTER TWELVE

## THE CHAKRA SYSTEM

Chakra is a Sanskrit word meaning, "wheel", perhaps because, to those who can see them, they look like wheels spinning. When Yoga practitioners practise their exercises, it is done to energise the main seven chakras, viz. root, sacral, solar-plexus, heart, throat, brow and crown. There are other major chakras viz. point-major ground (where the Earth energy enters the body at the feet, and the Auric top, about 12 inches above the head. Cosmic energy enters the body through this chakra. These two chakras are actively used in the practice of Qi Gung. There is also a chakra which points downwards from the groin-area to receive the energy, which is flowing up from the feet, making ten major chakras in all.

References to the chakras can be found, most notably, in the Hindu canonical literature, starting with the Upanishads. Chakras are also called lotuses or padmas. The Crown chakra is known as "the 1000 petalled lotus".

Chakras evolve naturally over a several lifetimes according to the spiritual development of the individual. It is said that ancient man had fewer chakra centres than modern man and that the solar plexus was the link to the supernatural.

The human body can be likened to an electrical appliance, which can only run when the appropriate energy is flowing through. Earth energy enters our bodies through the feet at place called, "bubbling spring" in acupuncture or the "foot-gate" in Qi-gung and other disciplines.(there are a number of "gates").

The energy flows from the entry-point to circulate the chakra system. As the energy reaches a chakra, some of the energy is drawn-off to feed certain organs or systems. The sacral chakra is. e.g. responsible for the water systems of the body, whereas the root is responsible for the bones and the chemical system.

The rest of the energy continues up through the system to the top of the aura where some is drawn-off to feed the auric-field before it continues down the other side of the body to exit beneath the feet.

Without the Earth-energy flowing through the body, we would die, and, it therefore, follows that if the chakra system is completely closed down, the same result would ensue. It is, therefore, not strictly accurate to talk about opening-up and closing down the chakras when doing spiritual or psychic work, but rather in activating the chakras and closing-off the aura with a protection layer or protecting the chakras with symbols, such as a silver cross. Silver is the age-old colour for protection; silver bullets were said to kill werewolves and the like). I prefer to cover the whole aura with silver.

It might seem strange at first, but even the Earth's energy is traced, ultimately, to cosmic energy. This is because all that exists comes from the same source, whether you consider that source to be God, (male or female), the cosmos, the universe or whatever.

However, earth energy is in a more concentrated form, and this is why some Eastern disciplines prefer to draw on cosmic energy. Taoists call this "The Water way". Using Earth energy is "The Fire way".

The "subtle bodies" seen around the physical body arise from "white light" but can be seen as components of this light; like light shining through a prism.

This can also be seen in the rainbow as the light from the Sun is spread across the sky. The colour of the chakra system is that of the rainbow. Beginning with the root as red to the crown, which is violet. Do not be concerned if you perceive the colours slightly differently to this, as it is perfectly normal.

Here is a list of the chakra basic chakra colours:

Point major ground (below and around the feet and ankles) silver

| | |
|---|---|
| **Root** | red |
| **Sacral** | orange |
| **Solar plexus** | yellow |
| **Heart** | green |
| **Throat** | sky blue |
| **Brow** | indigo (often seen more as a mauve) |
| **Crown** | violet (often seen more as a purple) |

**Auric top (Above the head) gold**

When the chakras are activated, they radiate different colours.

The following is a slightly more detailed account of the main chakras, including their Sanskrit titles and, where appropriate, the symbols associated with them as well as the vibratory rate of each chakra given as ---petalled lotus. e.g. the *four* petalled lotus gives a vibratory rate of 4.

ROOT (BASE) MULADHARA   EARTH   4 PETALLED LOTUS

SYMBOL: SQUARE   SENSE: SMELL   GLAND: ADRENALS / KIDNEYS

The root is responsible for the colon and rectum. This centre also controls the sense of smell. It links the body to the Earth. We can root ourselves through this point. It also controls body chemistry and nerve endings and the more solid elements of the physical body: bones, nails and teeth.

The root also provides energy for the reproductive system Lovemaking experienced through this chakra is very basic and lacking in tenderness and caring.

The root controls only some of the functions of the kidneys, viz. the ridding of waste matter.

## SACRAL (SVADISTHANA)   WATER   6 PETALLED LOTUS

SYMBOL: CRESCENT MOON    SENSE: TASTE

GLAND: TESTES / OVARIES / KIDNEYS

The sacral controls the fluid content of the body; the watery part of blood, saliva, tears, gland secretion etc. This centre is also involved in the reproductive and digestive systems; it is also involved with the emotions and gut-feeling psychic awareness and creativity.

Lovemaking using this chakra brings more emotional feelings into play

## SOLAR-PLEXUS (MANIPURA)   FIRE   10 PETALLED LOTUS

SYMBOL: TRIANGLE   SENSE: SIGHT   PANCREAS / SPLEEN

The solar plexus came in to being in primitive man in order to control the centres either side of it through the power of the mind. The solar plexus is also known as the "lower mind" and is associated with the intellect. It is the centre, which controls the chakras from the heart chakra downwards. The solar plexus sends energy to the digestive system, including the stomach, intestines, liver, spleen, pancreas etc. The SP is in control of the organs, which eliminate toxins from the system (liver and kidneys) the solar plexus used to known as the "fever point" because it is the centre, which combats disease, burning-out viruses and fighting infections.

The solar-plexus chakra is the exit point for astral travel.

## HEART (ANAHATA)   AIR   12 PETALLED LOTUS   SYMBOL: CIRCLE SENSE: TOUCH / THYMUS

Controls the respiratory system and the arterial system. The heart centre controls the emotions and is the seat of universal love. If it becomes blocked, the throat centre can also be affected. Crying and talking about problems can help to keep the chakras open and flowing.

Lovemaking from this chakra in conjunction with the sacral chakra will be tender, sensitive and true.

The heart chakra is the "gateway" to the higher chakras and it is best that this point be really clear before spiritual work is undertaken.

## THROAT (VISHUDDI)   ETHER   16 PETALLED LOTUS SYMBOL: OVOID   GLANDS: THYROID AND PARATHYROID SENSE: SOUND

The ether is the space in which the other elements operate. This centre when working well can make people talkative; it is the centre, which is predominant in singers. Arts and philosophy begin to take shape in this centre.

If feelings are bottled-up, then this point will, inevitably, become blocked.

This is the centre through which clairaudience is experienced.

## BROW (AJNA)   GLAND: PITUITARY 96P/L

This is the centre, which is involved in thinking processes; it is sometimes called the "higher mind". If this point is blocked, then thinking becomes muddled and thoughts keep going round and round in our minds.

The brow centre is associated with clairvoyance. If this centre is almost completely blocked, the person experiences the feeling of a tight band around the head.

## CROWN (SAHASRARA)   GLAND: PITUITARY

Although the vibratory rate of the crown is 960, it is known as the 1000 petalled lotus. This centre is our link with spirit and our over self. When we die, this is the point through which our spirit exits the body.

The chakras described above are the main energy centres. There are other, smaller centres all over the body. The points in the palms is where healing energy flows through and there are minor points at the elbows, wrists, the back of the knees and the ankles, to name but a few.

Most people teach that the heart centre is the seat of the emotions, but it is my belief that this is also true for the solar plexus, the sacral and the root. ( Indeed, all chakras are a seat of consciousness). You will all know that you get sensations in all of these areas due to different emotions. The closer to the ground, the more primitive the emotions. For example, extreme fear can lead to a soiling of the under garments. This might be through the action of the sacral or root chakra.

It is interesting, when listen to a piece of music, to feel stirrings in the different chakras as the music proceeds.

# CHAPTER THIRTEEN

## DEVELOPING MEDIUMSHIP

It is important, at this point, to know that there are three types of psychic: mediums, psychics and sensitives. Mediums, obviously, are those who can link in with Spirit to give evidence and to pass on messages. Psychics are people who can link into auras and read what is contained there. Sensitives are people with mediumistic abilities but can only work with the aid of their guides. Ivy Northage was the most famous of this type of mediumship. The late, great, Gordon Higginson refuted this classification until shortly before his death, when he wrote an article about it, confirming his belief in Mediums, psychics and sensitives.

It is also important to realize that mediumship, itself, relies on use of the psychic faculties. This is why many teachers include psychic exercises in their sessions: card readings, flower readings, coloured ribbon readings and the like. Developing the psychic senses will enable the medium to include the senses of smell and taste in their mediumship. For example, "I can taste apple pie, so this must be something that she liked/cooked". "I get a strong tobacco smell with him." These senses (they have special names) add colour and strength to the evidence.

Should you desire to become a medium, it is most beneficial to sit in a circle, which is already established and is run by a good medium. A circle is so-called because the old style mediums developed their mediumship sitting in a circular formation. This is because a circle affords the highest form of protection from mischievous spirits and untoward energies. Some of the old time mediums would draw a circle on the floor and mark-out the exact positions for the chairs to be placed. Modern mediums seem to be unaware of this, and allow people to sit in any old formation, on armchairs, settees and the like. Of course, they will say a prayer, at the beginning of the circle asking for protection and for the guides of all the sitters to join them.

Good circle controllers will interview prospective sitters to ascertain not only their motives for developing mediumship, but, also, whether or not the student will be able to attend regularly. This is especially important for people who need to get baby-sitters in order to attend circle. When I first sat in circle, controllers were most strict on this matter. These days there appears to be a lack of discipline, and sitters seem to come and go as they please, in some circles. If you wish to be a first class medium, discipline is of paramount importance.

Again, if the circle controller is experienced, you will be given a probationary period to see if the circle and the other sitters suit you and that you suit them. If at the end of that period, it has not worked-out, then you can leave the circle with no recriminations.

Discipline is essential for developing mediumship and, indeed, for treading the spiritual pathway in whatever forms it takes. This will involve arriving at the circle premises on time, (at least 15 minutes before the circle begins), refraining from talking about politics, religion or what a lousy day you've had. I get frustrated when circle leaders begin the evening by telling you to leave all the troubles of the day behind; and they do a little meditation to aid this. I have often been aware that people have arrived at the circle premises and have enjoyed chatting to the other people in the circle, completely forgetting the cares of the day in the excitement of the evening, only to be reminded of it by the circle controller at the beginning of the circle.

Be warned, not all good mediums are good teachers. I have sat in circle with some of the best mediums in my home locality. Some were good at teaching, others, were not, and some were very dictatorial in their approach, not accepting that everyone works differently. One medium told us that if we didn't ask Spirit questions, they wouldn't speak to us. In all the times I have been on the platform, I have never asked the communicator a question: I have, however, primed my guide beforehand as to what evidence I would like to give and they have, in turned, primed the communicator. As Eamonn Downey says, let Spirit say what they have come to say. If we ask too many questions, we are dictating to Spirit; they know what they want to say, I just ask for two or three pieces of evidence as proof of survival and to find the recipient quickly.

It is possible for someone who is, perhaps, not such a good medium, to be a good teacher. It is said that one should sit with a particular medium for only two years. This is individual, of course, but you can gain a wider experience by sitting with different mediums. Don't, however, flit from one circle to another.

When I first sat in circle, it was common practice to "open up the chakras" to enable the sitters to work, psychically and mediumistically. These days, it is more common to "widen" the aura and to set the intention to link in with Spirit. Whatever works for you is valid. However it is done, the purpose is to raise your vibrations and to, partially, disassociate yourself from the material plane. It is always vital to put the conscious mind to one side whilst engaging in mediumship, so don't try to interpret what you are seeing, hearing or feeling. Just give off what comes to you. It will make sense to the recipient. If they are unsure, go back to Spirit and ask them to show you more clearly or specifically.

Beginners will usually be talked through "guided visualizations". This is not the same as "meditation". Guided visualizations ask the sitters to imagine a short journey, usually along a pathway. Often you start in a meadow of some kind and are asked to see, in the mind, grass, flowers etc. Frequently, there is a gate to open or a stile to step over before you see the pathway.

You will be taken on a mind journey to a specific place and given time to stay in that place. Often, you are told that there is a person in that place; either a guide or a member of your family who is in the Spirit world. You are given time to examine the place or to talk to whoever is with you. After a while you are guided back to the circle room; frequently bringing back, (symbolically), something that Spirit have given you. This might be an object such as a gem- stone or a message of guidance.

The main reasons for this type of exercise are: to help to exercise the imagination, (which is very important in mediumship) and to train sitters in discipline. A lot of mediumship involves seeing images in the Mind's eye. Seeing a spirit for example or seeing a scene and the like. Being disciplined in following the instructions, given in the visualization helps to focus the mind while working. For example, it is possible to describe the spirit you are seeing, with reference to build, age dress, etc. Memories are often conveyed through the scenes, which a spirit might pass to the medium.

The next important reason is to develop general discipline. In one circle in which I sat, one of the sitters never once followed the instructions of the circle controller in the visualizations. Obviously, she was not disciplined in her daily life, which was true, and this can lead to all sorts of problems. It is essential, if one is to fulfil the innate potential to its limits, to be disciplined.

Good circle controllers will help sitters to understand the meaning of what has been seen in the visualization. Sitters can get frustrated, when, having been given something from Spirit, do not understand it. The controller, will link in with the sitter's guide to reveal the meaning.

Guided visualization is usually the basic beginner's exercise. This can be followed, by doing psychic readings for other members of the circle. This might entail the holding of the other person's hands, linking in via the solar plexus, chakras or auras or by holding an object belonging to the person: Psychometry. In these exercises, the medium tries to pick up what is going on in the person's life at that moment. Not specifically, but pick up on the emotions or mood. Of course this can be enlarged later on, but no detailed circumstances must be revealed in front of others. Where sitters are partnered by another person, and there is space enough, it is possible to be a little more specific. Something like, "There is a problem in your life at the moment which makes you angry, but you are managing to not lose your temper". That is specific enough.

Meditation is, properly, making contact with the inner-self; your own spirit; there are many ways to achieve this, such as repeating a mantra. Usually this is something like Om Mani Padme Hum. In simple terms, this is the mantra of compassion. Padme means, lotus and signifies the Lotus family of all the Buddhas. It is the shortened version of, Padmasambhava. There are many such mantras from the Orient. You can, of course, make up your own mantra using your own language. Something like, "I sit in the power of Spirit".

Some people use a yantra for meditation. A yantra is a visual object. The simplest yantra is a hollow circle, drawn on a sheet of paper. More complicated yantras are the symbol of Ohm and the yin-yang symbol. This sort of meditation is not part of the regime for budding mediums, although, it may be practiced separately. When I attended yoga classes, for the meditation part of the evening, we had to stare at a lighted candle for several minutes and then hold that image in our minds as we closed our eyes.

The ultimate mantra is OM/AUM. This is the mantra connecting us to the Supreme Being; the universal consciousness. It is a mantra of great power when intoned properly. The sound should begin at the back of the throat, move to the middle of the mouth and the mm sound should be at the front. I heard this performed by a group of young women at Avesbury and it was an awesome experience as I could feel the energy building up within the group, and spreading outwards. It is best to be taught by an experienced practitioner.

A practice, which is very beneficial, in the development of mediumship, is, "Sitting in the power". Some might consider this to be similar to meditation. It involves becoming aware of your own spirit and your own place in the universe. Some consider it to be linking with the Universal Consciousness.

It is beneficial for improving your mediumship and also your very being. As Tony Stockwell says, "it feeds the Soul". There are several different CDs on the market, devoted to this exercise. A very popular one is by Tony Stockwell (on the CD "Heighten Your Spiritual Awareness"), but there are others. Notably by Glynn Edwards and Martin Twycross.

It would be foolish of me to try to explain any further; these versions of "Sitting in the power" all explain themselves. All I can say is that the practice is one of the most beneficial that you can undertake.

Having spent some time in circle developing your mediumship, it is a good idea to try it out on friends and family. Set aside an half hour for this purpose.

It will boost your confidence as you improve. Of course, the good circle controller will have invited guests to the circle on whom the sitters will practise. Then there are, so-called, 'Fledgling' evenings where the new mediums will practise on people whom they might not know. These sessions can take place in the controller's home or in a Spiritualist church.

One of the mistakes made these days is for mediums to start their practice before they are truly ready. The circle leader should tell the mediums when they are ready. Starting out too early can lead to very poor standards of mediumship. This has been very evident when someone has put them self, forward to serve a church or do private sittings. Like most other things, mediumship is a life long learning process. If someone thinks that they've "arrived" after a couple of years in circle, they couldn't be more wrong.

Mediumship improves year on year with use and the evidence becomes more detailed and involved. It is most important to remain humble whatever level you reach. Remember, you are serving God and Spirit; you are but a channel for their purpose. Ego serves no purpose in mediumship. Acknowledge your gifts by all means but remember, the word is gift: it can be taken away.

One medium that I knew told us that he had to sit in his development circle for seven years before the circle leader allowed him and fellow students to demonstrate to the public. These days, people often appear on platforms after a couple of years but that is only the beginning. It is a fact that the power in circles aids mediumship through the combined energies of the controller and sitters. Therefore, when the medium appears in public for the first time, they are usually not as good as they were in circle conditions.

I know this from personal experience. Building confidence and exercising their mediumship through public demonstrations will improve the quality of their work. Like an athlete preparing for a race, warming-up and exercising the mediumship muscle, will improve performance.

One of the aids to good mediumship is having a wide knowledge. Spirit can access the knowledge stored in our brains to give specific information to recipients. For example, knowing the names of such things as flowers, cars, countries, cities names of streets, medical knowledge, breeds of dogs etc. can be used to verify the identity of the communicating spirit. Of course, first names and surnames are very useful.

For example, " I have a lady here who used to own a (specific make of) car. She loved the countryside, especially when the bluebells were in bloom.

She had a Pekinese dog and a Siamese cat. She mentions the city of Liverpool and also Bolton. She loved her garden in which she grew delphiniums, roses and pansies. She's telling me her name is Jane and she is an aunt to somebody Here.

You can see that such information is useful to pinpoint the identity of the communicator. We were told to memorize lists of such things as flowers, breeds of dogs etc. As a musician, at one stage of my mediumship, I was given the words of songs in my messages. Another time, I heard the words, 'Shanklin, Isle of Wight, clairaudiently", and the lady recipient exclaimed, "That's where we had our honeymoon".

The information might come to you clairaudiently or clairvoyantly. If you recognize some things by sight it could be given to you through your clairvoyance, if you know things by their names, however, it will probably be given to you through your clairaudience.

It is always important to say what you see. It can be very frustrating when mediums try to interpret what they are seeing or hearing. Often, they do this without asking the communicator to clarify. This has been dealt with in a previous chapter. On one occasion, I had someone's aunt with me, and she was showing me coins, which she poured from one hand to the other. I could have made a wild guess at what this meant but I didn't. I just said, "Well, she keeps repeating this action". The gentleman then recalled that his aunt had been an accountant. It's a peculiar way of showing her profession but I was pleased that I didn't try to interpret the action and be very wide of the mark.

Once you have built the ability to give good "evidence", it is essential to link into Spirit, clairsentiently. Mediumship, of course, varies from person to person, and it is possible to begin your mediumship as a clair- sentient. In which case, it is important to be as specific as you can because it is easy to give, "woolly" messages if you just have vague feelings. Once clair-sentience is firmly established it can produce the best evidence of the persona of the communicator. I love this form of mediumship when the blending is so close that you almost become the communicator and can speak and gesture with their mannerisms. Such mediumship can bring them "back to life" in the mind of the recipient. One of my teachers, (Eamonn Downey), used to call me the "arm chair" medium because, he said, my messages were like being in the room with the communicator and having a chat with them.

As stated in the previous paragraph, the development of mediumship is individual. The good circle controller will encourage you to develop the gift that you have. If your mediumship begins with clairsentience, it is wrong of the controller to try to get you to bring through such things as names of flowers or house numbers etc. Mediumship tends to change with use and practice. You might begin with clairvoyance and then move to, or add, clairaudience. It is quite common for this to happen; usually, you end up with all the "clairs", including clair-cognizance (clair-knowing). This is where you find yourself just speaking and giving-off a lot of information without even thinking about it. This comes when you have achieved the ability to blend very closely with Spirit. It is always essential to set your intention before trying to communicate with Spirit. Of course, this should be set by the circle controller, but it's always a good thing to ask Spirit to communicate with you and to ask your guides to direct the message. This saves a lot of fishing around at the beginning of the message. Ask for such things as name, passing condition, occupation etc.

Some mediums like their sitters to direct, that is, state your intention to go to a particular person. I found this easy in circle but not so easy in a church or hall with a sea of faces staring at you. If you are moved to direct, then do so; if you are not, work indirectly. That is, give out some evidence that will be accepted by one person. Sometimes, more than one person can accept the evidence and it is the job of the medium to ask Spirit for some specific information that only one person can accept. I have found over the years, that most of the people who direct are, in fact, working psychically. They often dress it up as mediumship, so it is difficult to tell at times. Sometimes, they begin with a psychic link and then link in to Spirit, mediumistically.

Often, their direction is prompted by something about the person, which catches their attention. The person might cough, or blow their nose; sometimes attention is drawn by something that a person is wearing.

We often hear something like, "I'm coming to the lady wearing the lovely purple scarf. I don't know what I've got yet". Good mediums wait for a communicator to come through with evidence that only one person can accept.

It is best to put yourself forward to work as a medium only when you have been producing good evidence in circle for quite a while. As stated previously, some controllers invite guests for their students to work with.

This is a very good practice because, if sitters get to know each other too well, memory can come into play. The student medium must be fully confident in circle before they venture forth into the world of mediumship.

This is because the energies in circle enable sitters to work much more easily than in a church or hall. Everyone in the circle is, usually, mediumistic and is rooting for their fellow sitters. In churches and halls, the situation is very different. Sometimes, the medium has to fight to keep the energies high and flowing. There's usually some negativity somewhere in the audience and always, there are people who are, 'message grabbers'. These people will pull on the energy of the medium to get a message for themselves. Frequently, these people get a message every time they attend a meeting. They are the bane of the medium and the congregation. Sometimes they will 'bend' the evidence in a ridiculous way, in order to get a message. The thing is, that often, their loved one from Spirit will barge in front of the communicator who is having difficulty in giving off the exact evidence which will identify them and the recipient. This might be because they are new to communicating, (it is a skill which they have to learn), or they could be having difficulty because of their emotions. Message grabbers usually have seasoned communicators who know how to push themselves forward. It is a good thing to start the message with some good, specific information, which will pinpoint the communicator; this will enable the correct recipient to answer-up and put paid to the message grabbers.

When you are new to the platform you will find that there is always someone who will try to tell you how to work. Frequently, this is a would-be medium who couldn't do what you are doing but wants to convince you that they could, if they wanted to. You have to be polite but try to indicate that you know what you are doing and that you work in your own, individual way.

Don't be put off by such people; feel sorry for them and send them thoughts for enlightenment.

It is easy to say, but enjoy your mediumship. Beginners are often terrified when they stand up in front of a crowd of people. I often give a little talk before I launch into the mediumship because I do feel a bit awkward waiting for Spirit to come through. The last time I was on the platform, I recited some of my inspired poetry whilst Spirit came in on the energy of that. Most mediums actually give a talk about how they work before they do their first communication.

Mediumship is very rewarding for the medium. I consider that it is a form of healing for those who are grieving or those who need upliftment. Most mediums will tell you that Spirit will not tell you what to do but, sometimes, a little timely advice will be of great help to someone in need. The most essential thing is not to be prescriptive. In other words, don't tell people what to do and in particular, don't tell anyone that they have a health problem or to ditch their partner. You can get into a lot of trouble doing things like that. You can make oblique references, however and leave the recipients to make up their own mind.

There is a great need for good mediums, so, take the bit between your teeth and tell Spirit that you would like to work in this wonderful way.

# CHAPTER FOURTEEN

## YOUR PERSONAL JOURNEY

Everybody's spiritual journey is individual; it is particular to them.

Of course, they will learn from other people, from books and, perhaps, addresses in the Spiritualist church, or seminars given by, hopefully, people who are more advanced than they. It is advisable always to be aware that there are those, out there, who are out to make money out of you. Your own common sense and innate spiritual knowledge will help you here to discriminate fact from fiction.

As I have stated before, the most important person in your life is you, yourself, so, make time for yourself amid the hurly-burly of life. If you are sincerely desirous of working for and with Spirit, then give yourself the time that you, and they, deserve. At the sanctuary where my wife and I trained as healers and mediums, the founders used to talk about the "three Ds"; desire, dedication and discipline. Without these three things, your journey, at best, will be spasmodic. I remember, many years ago, when I was a group leader in "The Fountain Group". A young woman who hadn't been to the group for several months bounced in at one of the main meetings of TFG, gushing with, "When is the next meeting; I want to do something spiritual"? I told her that I had suspended the group because few of the people in the group wanted to do any more than just turn up for meetings and be spoon-fed. "If you wish to do something spiritual, I told her, go to the Spiritualist church and develop in a circle there", but you must be disciplined and turn up every week. She disappeared from my radar after that.

If you have responsibilities in your everyday life, these are important but you must decide how exactly important they are. Often, we think that things are more important than they, in reality, are.

Having decided which things take paramount position in your life, then you can find time within your schedule to devote to your spiritual development; that is, to devote to yourself. Before people were permitted to join our sanctuary, they were given rigorous interviews where all the officers were present to judge the applicant and to ask individual questions. One of the important questions was, "Will you be able to attend every week"? If they were unable to commit, they were denied a place. Some leeway was always granted in special cases. Parents with young children had to make sure that baby-sitting was arranged for the whole of the course before they started with us.

You might be glad to know that things are, usually, not so rigorous these days.

So, you have the desire (to heal or do mediumship etc.) and the dedication; that is, you have dedicated yourself to turning up every week, (or fortnight) for the period of the course. Now, you must make sure that you are disciplined. Always turn up at the stated time, be quiet when asked and obey all the rules. Whilst sitting in circle, always pay heed to the circle controller. If you find it difficult not to fidget, then, perhaps, just sitting at home meditating will have to be your beginning. After a while, you might find that you are able to sit for longer. One group, in which I sat, regularly sat "in the power" for almost an hour. When you achieve that depth of attunement, it is quite easy to sit for that long; unless there are physical problems, which prevent it. (My wife used to take a cushion with her if she knew that the seats would be uncomfortable).

One question, which came up frequently, is, "Am I too old to start developing"? The answer is, of course, you are never too old. Remember what I said about spiritual age in an earlier chapter, Spirit does not age. Moreover, what we learn in this life is carried forward to the next one; so, learn as much as you can in this life to give you a flying start in the next.

I cannot re-iterate enough that "The most important person in your life is you, yourself". It is your journey that you are here to travel. Before you came to the Earth you set yourself certain goals to reach. It would be a shame that they are not achieved because other things or people, got in the way'. Look after yourself first; this gives you the strength and energy to look after others.

In looking after yourself, it is essential to consider diet. I am not a nutritionist, but I will eat, only organic food because I feel that my body is not equipped to deal with the herbicides and pesticides, which are sprinkled over crops. I try, also, to follow, as near as possible, an alkaline diet. The body requires a diet that leaves a slight residue of alkali. Our food intake should be 60/40 in favour of alkali. To maintain homeostasis, the body will borrow calcium from other parts of the system. The alkaline diet is recommended by Nutritionists, and others in the "Alternative" field, but some doctors say that the diet does not aid the alkalinity of the system. However, they do concede that the diet is a good diet in that it promotes the ingestion of fruits, vegetables and nuts.

Healthy exercise is good for you; preferably something that you enjoy rather than something which has to be endured, and so negates the beneficial effects. Always seek professional advice before embarking on an exercise regime. Yoga, Tai Chi and chi gung are very good exercise regimes. I practised Yoga for about twenty years and then switched to Tai Chi and Chi gung.

These three practises will all aid your mediumship as well as promoting a healthy body.

If you wish to take up healing, then it is usually required to take a course. Such courses can last from about nine months to two years dependant upon the association, which you join.

A practice, which I found very beneficial, is 'chakra clearing'. At our sanctuary, we spent a year doing it every week in circle and every day at home. The practice involves drawing down white light from the cosmos and channelling it through the chakras. I think it is best to start from the root because, if you clear from the brow, downwards, then when all the channels to the upper chakras are clear, then "dirty" energy from the root could rise upward and that is unadvisable. It is a slow process but well worth taking the time. You can sit on a chair to do this, visualising the energy coming down through the crown to the bottom of the spine and then through each chakra. Spend as long as it takes to clear the first chakra before moving to the next; although as the root clears you can clear the sacral concurrently. This practice can also be performed lying down, but breathing cosmic energy through the feet, through the chakra at the perineum and thence to the chakras located at the spine. (The chakras flow through the spine both ways into the aura). When the trunk chakras are clear, then do the Point Major Ground, followed by the Crown. The lower chakra extends below the feet and there is also the point above the crown to be cleared. As the chakras begin to clear, their proper colours will begin to appear.

Development circles are abundant; they might be attached or affiliated to a Spiritualist church or be entirely independent. It is usual to hear of such a circle through a friend. Be prepared for anything; some circles are excellent and some are not so good. If you are a complete beginner, then you have no yardstick. Don't give up entirely if the first circle you join is not to your liking; there will always be one which will suit you. Be prepared to accept everything as an experience. Nothing that is experienced is ever a waste of time. Experiencing different circles and people, will help you to discriminate, and you will experience different ways of doing things. As I said before, changing circles is one thing but do not hop from one to another.

Whatever you read or learn in any other way, your inner voice will guide you as to what is right or wrong for you. Sometimes, you will change your opinions about certain things as you develop.

As stated previously, never think, "Oh, I've arrived". The best medium I know is continually progressing. I've been to several of his courses and workshops and they are always different. Remember the Spiritualist's 7th Principal: "Eternal progress open to every human soul". So, be prepared for change as you make progress. This change in you can effect your life outside of your spiritual work; you are likely to lose old friends who are not interested in what you are doing and gain new friends who are of a like mind. Your attitudes to various things in your life can also change; you might be more tolerant of some things and less tolerant of others.

You might start of with a clear idea that you wish to heal the sick or give messages of comfort to those in distress but as you develop more and more, you realise that you are serving a higher purpose. The work that you do will be a 'Service' to God, Spirit and Mankind. Always bear that in mind when working so as to keep the ego in its place. Ego is necessary to work in public but keep it under control or your work will suffer. Which leads me to: never put limits on yourself. Unfortunately, we are often curtailed in our youth, by people putting limits on us. Sometimes this comes about because of the way that we were treated at school, and sometimes through different associations which we have as we are growing up. So, place into your subconscious, the thought "I can do anything" and then just accept your work as it comes. Sometimes, you will shine, and sometimes, for one reason or another, your work will not be so good.

Some teachers are fond of giving their students affirmations or get them to make up their own. This is a good practice for getting students to be positive about their capabilities.

My mother was always telling me not to 'show-off'. Which has probably led to my reluctance in pushing myself forward in anything. I sometimes think of myself as "The reluctant medium" because it takes a lot to get me onto the platform although I enjoy it when I'm there. My wife and I started of with no other purpose than to heal. During our first course, we discovered that developing our mediumship would make us better healers. From that limited vision of what we would do, I have branched out into working on the platform, (mainly to promulgate my own brand of philosophy), composing music, given to me by Spirit, writing poetry and in writing this book.

Always be aware that your work is a privilege and is a service, not only to Mankind but to Spirit and to God, (however you perceive God to be). You are representing Spirit when you put yourself forward, so work to the very best of your ability; even when, perhaps, there are problems in your private life, or someone has upset you. Put the outside world to rest when you are working but if you feel unable to do that at that moment, it is best to withdraw and get a stand-in.

The main things to remember are: be positive, KNOW, that you are capable and enjoy working with Spirit and with the different energies, which you will recognise as your experience grows.

If you have administered healing to someone or given them a message, always accept their thanks courteously and without ego. Never do what I have witnessed many times from mediums; shout, "Don't thank me, it's them upstairs". A healer that I once knew used to do this and I used to think, "He's just undone all the good of the healing". This person was one of the most genuine of spirit workers with whom it's been my pleasure to work, but it does show an ignorance of spirit law. We have to remember, that we are essential to the process; without us, Spirit would be unable to do their work. If someone came to me for healing and I said, "Just sit there on that seat and Spirit will give you healing. I'm going into the other room to have a cup of tea", the patient would probably bolt out of the door. Working with Spirit is an equal partnership and helps them with their spiritual progress as well as you with yours. Even our guides have others over them who supervise their progress.

To deny the part that you play in healing or clairvoyant- mediumship, demeans your own work and place in the partnership. Remember, people want to thank you; they have a need to thank you. Don't throw it back in their face and thus cause negative energy. So, respect this need and just reply quietly something to the effect, "It's a pleasure".

As mentioned previously, "Sitting in the Power" is perhaps, the singular best technique, which you can practise, so I recommend it strongly right from the start. If your teacher observes this practice, then you are off to a flying start; if not, then look into the CDs mentioned earlier.

I do hope that the afore going will be useful to you as you make you spiritual journey, but remember, it is your journey and what suits you is individual to you.

You make take parts of it or even adjust some of it to suit your own self and remember, "You are the most important person in your life".